Rainbow for Arid

A book that sheds light on developmental

modules that must be considered

to liberate Africa from economic hardship

and create a view of Africa

that display a fortified,

rich and unified continent.

By

Enoch Kwarteng

DEDICATION

To Africans and every student ready to significantly impact their lives and enhance mental and social development in Africa and the world.

EPIGRAPH

I am not African because I was born in Africa ……..but because Africa was born in me.

Dr Kwame Nkrumah

ACKNOWLEDGEMENTS

The starting point of anything relevant mostly requires help from others to support one move from a point toward achieving one's dream or an instrument that will assist one in drawing the point to mark one's dreams' orientation. Consequently, the birth of this great piece results from the contributions of people who supported this course with words of encouragement and professional assistance. This piece is more or less a research work designed to find solutions to Africa's most pressing problems to aid in pulling Africa's destiny from the stagnation which has been the common narrative. As a result, research was conducted from the grass root within the African community to understand the problems at the primary level, which positively impacted the writing process.

Most importantly, my gratitude goes to God for His grace. My gratitude goes to those who supported me in the process of this book to completion. Also, I thank my parents for being my best role models. George Jamel Kwarteng, my brother, phenomenally impacted my growth. I remember during my school days. He would buy self-help books, hand them to me to read and give me a deadline to complete them. My failure to meet such a deadline meant I would be denied anything materialistic that I asked for. Consequentially, all these efforts of my brother prepared me to be an author; as they say, "readers become leaders."

The propitiation and patriotism of the forefathers of Independence Africa who fought for Independence and liberated the land is not only a history but also a reminder that constantly kept me on my toes not to botch up their good works for the toil of their blood to label me as a foe to the African soil, my pride. Gratitude is not enough to Pan Africanists who have left a good example as a reference for African descent to emulate to achieve the African dream.

Chris Agyeman, Feisel Kwarteng, and Richard Osei Appiah (brothers), who ensured that I became the better version of myself, deserve my appreciation. I thank Dr Emmanuel Kwateng Drokow, a brother I met at Zhengzhou University, for his professional support and Mr Hamis Kiggundu, a Ugandan businessman, for inspiring Africa over the years. I am grateful to Dr Michael Oppong, a Dental Surgeon at Presbyterian Hospital, Agogo. He encouraged me by sharing his experiences with me, as he always tells me he wishes to see my growth. For the quantum words of encouragement I received from my relatives and friends, Ernestina Akua Osaah, Shilla Agyabeng Nti, Dorothy Agyeman, Emmanuel Afoakwa, James Owusu, Najat Kwarteng, Yasmin Kwarteng, Rhoda Agyeman, Mrs Naomi Agyemang, Yaw Sarpong and Mr Ahmed Amponsah Fordjour; they were beneficial and propelled me higher to put on the fabric of silver-lining to push forward and not give up.

Finally, I thank my editorial and designing team, Beloved Publishing House, Doris Foster, Jeremise Oduro, Kingsman Owusu Ansah, Opoku Peprah, Emmanuella Nti, Felicia Okyerebea, John Paul Rugaba, and Eugene

Edzeafene-Mensah. The motivation I got from all the people mentioned above is well appreciated.

CONTENTS

FOREWORD

In the movie "the last samurai", Algren had quite a profound perception of the Samurai; They are intriguing people. From the moment they wake, they devote themselves to the perfection of whatever they pursue. I have never seen such discipline. I am surprised to learn that the word Samurai means 'to serve'.

Algren would have a similar perception about Akwasi Kwarteng, the boy child from Suame magazine, who applied himself diligently in all his endeavours. Akwasi remained resolute even in the noisy environment of Suame magazine(an engineering hub in Kumasi, Ghana), took what he could from his environment, and made the most he could from life.

Akwasi, the sad traveller, has heartfelt yearnings to see the development and progression of the African continent. A sad traveller because, through the streets of China to the beautiful European cities, Akwasi notices the stark contrast between where his umbilical cord was buried and where His feet walk now.

As the sages put it, Africa has its natural disasters in bad leadership, corruption, cronyism, nepotism, and tribalism, just to mention a few. The ripple effects of our versions of natural disasters cause damages in quantities and magnitude more than hurricanes and earthquakes leave behind.

Even though Akwasi held the gun, I have been in the trenches with him, directing and supporting him; he has crafted these beautiful chapters.

Akwasi, in this beautiful book, albeit with ink from his tears, directs the Africans to see their worth, believe that they are capable, and have a mental orientation to reduce the ugly African natural disasters.

Dr Michael Oppong, MD, is a Dental Surgeon

at Presbyterian Hospital, Agogo and an entrepreneur.

PREFACE

The African community has always been highlighted as the land of the ages. However, Africa's liberty in most crucial aspects of life seems to have been caged over the years. The African soil has been a substantial venture that has benefited the world immensely regarding rich resources, epitomizing the land. Beautiful vegetation, rivers, oceans, and minerals spread across the continent supposedly make the environment and the inhabitants robust by default. Most Africans need to realize the natural finery their skin displays and the corresponding apparel of opulence covering the continent.

Dragging the bigger picture down the African memory lane, not only have the natural resources of the African soil benefited the world, but most African scholars have also made phenomenal impacts. Even though Africa has excellent and creative minds, the environment must be more conducive to supporting such talents. Many African scholars seek greener pastures elsewhere to hone their creative skills and positively influence science and technology. If the African community focuses on their identity to know their capabilities, innovations and creativity will reach their climax.

According to the Europeans, civilization started in Greece. Isocrates, an ancient Greek rhetorician, stated in a book titled Busiris that he studied medicine in Egypt. This statement by Isocrates implies that there are a lot of products, knowledge, and resources that the average African can explore and materialize towards her growth. Below are examples of Africans who have impacted the world positively with their skill, knowledge, and talent.

Hatim Zaghloul, an Egyptian born in Giza, invented WIFI with his long-time friend Dr Michel Fattouche in wideband orthogonal frequency division, multiplexing, and multi-code direct-sequence spread spectrum.

Iddris Sandu, born in Accra, Ghana, and residing in Los Angeles, is an architectural technologist who created the world's first retail store experience along with Nipsey Hussle, according to HanDWIKI. He has also developed algorithms for Instagram, Snapchat, and Uber.

Mary Spio, a Ghanaian-born deep space engineer, tech innovator, and entrepreneur, founded creations like CEEK Virtual Reality and currently holds four patents, one allowing for the digital transfer of Star Wars. She has designed and launched satellites into deep space on a NASA project. She subsequently became the head of satellite communication systems for Boeing Corporation.

Disheartening, countless creative Africans have been impoverished due to bad governance. This yearning is the wake-up call that propelled me to ruminate on how the common narrative of African society can be changed into a more refreshing and appealing subject that resonates with the African mind's true self. To cultivate the fruit that the African soil is designed to produce to sustain her people, I planned to plant seeds in a garden that would free the Africans from being destitute and allow them to enjoy their natural blessings. In addition, I wrote a self-help book titled "Wisdom is the New Swag,' a book that aims to fix the mind on primary life expectancy and guides one to reconsider the need to consciously develop oneself in health and wealth, factoring in their mental, emotional, and social development. This book aims to positively fix one's mind to awaken oneself and defend one's territory with wisdom. As the mind is a powerful tool that is a platform for the orientation of arguably everything, it was necessary to produce a piece that aims to lead one on the path of reasoning to make one mentally strong and emotionally sturdy. In addition, I published another book titled 'ECHOES OF THE SLEEPING GIANT.' It is a book filled with personal experiences and realities that clearly show how China reasoned her way out of economic hardship. It also touches on modules and effective practices that have contributed to the development of China and Asia. These can be applied in Africa to effect positive change, according to my lens of experience. Cementing all these write-ups aimed at enhancing a quality mindset to yield growth to achieve the garden, Africa needs to conclude this write-up you are about to   explore.

RAINBOW FOR ARID

CHAPTER 1
INTRODUCTION

Crossing respective African borders in the dead of night within a brainwork by utilizing African history as an illumination reveals Africa as a mother continent. The African continent has accommodated humans for more than 5 million years. The mother continent (Africa) is the second-largest continent, bounded by the Mediterranean Sea, the Red Sea, the Indian Ocean, and the Atlantic Ocean. Even though the African community consists of different countries with various tribes having unique cultures, looking deep into historical traces suggests they must have originated from a shared cultural heritage. This variety accounts for the screaming most African leaders and Pan-Africanists have expressed in their scholarly writings. These aim to establish a united Africa to enhance growth. Africa has significant natural resource wealth, home to the world's largest arable landmass, the second-largest and longest rivers (the Nile and the Congo), and its second-largest tropical forest.

Despite all these resources with precious minerals that sweep the African continent, Africa's underdeveloped state is a paradox complicated to comprehend and painful to relate to as an African. Candidly, this problem constantly pushes ordinary Africans to give up and live without hope and a future. However, the hopeful reality is that there is no problem without a cause, so if the cause of the impoverished state of Africa is being addressed and dealt with seriously with solutions, then the hope to see the sunlight the following day when one sleeps in the evening will be a rhyming synonym for Africa.

According to Komla Tsey in his book titled "Re-thinking Development in Africa," if Africa's rich oral traditions are propagated and encouraged for ordinary Africans to embrace and relate to, it will enhance the appreciation of African cultures by her people by utilizing story-sharing as a research methodology. Thus, the ordinary African can visualize oneself in African history with an unquenchable urge to seek and design a way to proceed into the future. (Tsey, K. 2011). Re-thinking Development in Africa

This book focuses on the happenings within the tunnels in Africa, causes for maximization of her problems, and solutions to create light within the tunnel rather than the promised light at the tunnel's end, which one cannot be sure of. In addition, developmental modules to make the ordinary African feel proud of oneself, appreciate one's culture and take one's destiny at heart with great effort and work are included in this write-up. In a broader sense, it informs the African Community to focus on modules and cultures that bring out a more refined mind to fight constructively for success, as the hope and vision are to fix the African community. Succinctly, Africa has displayed a particular alluring narrative over the century; this piece aims to discuss ways to colour the ancient monochrome to give a view of Africa that symbolizes unity, growth, and freedom at all levels. In tandem, this book concludes with unappealing practices that the African Community has held firmly, affecting her development from a psychological standpoint.

AN INSIGHT INTO AFRICA

One glance at the world map and among many other distinct features, one stands out. At the centre is a huge mass of a continent second only to Asia in the land mass crisscrossed by all central latitudes and longitudes. Early explorers once described that continent as dark and, by some 20th-century Western economies, as a failed state of investment. The continent, just like the morning sun, has risen above this bias. Ladies and gentlemen, I present to you Africa, the cradleland of humankind.

When the first humans evolved and set foot from the great East African savannah, little did they know that they would become the most dominant species on the planet for the next million years. And if you are not a believer in evolution, then there is undoubtedly no place on earth that is currently the biblical representation of the Garden of Eden like Africa. A continent so blessed by the heavens that beneath lies a treasure vault of minerals beyond human imagination. 1 in 8 people in the world is African. But be not deceived that Africa is homogenous. Africa is a collection of over 5000 ethnicities with over 1000 distinct languages spoken on the continent. Over the past 100 years, news from Africa has been mainly dictated by negative stereotypes such as war, famine, drought, etc.; they neglect the ever-present but vibrant warmth of the African smile.

The Empires on The African Continent

Over the past 5000 years, large and successful empires have called Africa home. The most well-known are those established at the banks of Africa's great rivers, such as Ancient Egypt on the Nile and the empire of Mali on the banks of river Niger. Much as the story of ancient Egypt is well documented, it still serves as a typical example of the greatness of human civilisation, especially in the harsh terrain of the desert. From wonders such as the pyramids of Giza to sites such as the Valley of the Kings, ancient Egypt is a classic example of what great man can achieve as a collective unit. Further southwest, there was an empire that will forever remain in the hearts of many. The kingdom of Mali was made famous by its vast wealth and power, lest we forget its favourite son Mansa Musa. Mansa Musa, arguably the wealthiest person to have ever lived, is a prime example of African wealth and prosperity despite the standard narrative that some media push today that he isn't. The city of Timbuktu, in the empire, was the cradleland of education on the continent some 500 years before Western education arrived on the continent. This period of African history can be classified as the golden era. Many scientists, doctors, traders, mathematicians, religious scholars, and even great explorers like Ibn Battuta flourished during this period.

Further south, societies such as the Kingdom of Ghana and the Empire of Benin flourished. The empire of Benin was well known for its magnificent bronze works that caught the eye of the colonialists that eventually looted the kingdom of its wealth. The Chwezi empire in the great lakes region was also a great society that introduced skills such as iron making, backcloth making, coffee growing, etc., as well as a centralised system of governance that later evolved into great kingdoms such as Buganda, Bunyoro, Ankole, and Karagwe.

In southern Africa, the great societies of Great Zimbabwe were made famous for their great Zimbabwe stone works and the vast gold wealth of the kingdom of Mutapa. But no club in southern Africa is more renowned as the mighty empire of the Zulus. Founded by its famous son, shaka zulu, this era describes the warrior and military genius of African societies. Military tactics developed by the Zulu state under shaka, such as the cow–horn formation, have been redeployed in various ways over the years in many subsequent military conflicts.

Last but not least, it's fair to say that modern Africa is shaped by the ancient empires that ruled over the vast continent to this very day.

1800 TO PRESENT.

Everyone is well familiar with the slave trade and its evils. Whether the blame is attributed to the Europeans and the Arabs that carried it out or the African chiefs who sold their compatriots for mirrors and clothes, history will judge best. However, the effects of slavery still live with us to this very day in the African mindset, such as the African mentality of mutual distrust and self-centred success rather than collective success. Other profound legacies of this period are the vast African diaspora in the Caribbean and the Americas who have gone on to do great works. But the greatest evil this period left on the continent was the underdevelopment it caused because non-disabled people were all shipped out.

Fast forward to the scramble to Africa, where the continent was divided among great European powers like a piece of cake. Despite the onset of colonialism, great African leaders stood up and Faught for their values and dignity, leaders such as Yaa Asantewaa of the Ashanti, made famous for the Ashanti -British wars, and emperor of Menelik who defeated the Italians at the battle of Adwa. And if slavery was the worst we saw of foreign domination, then the deaths of 60 million Congolese by King Leopold of Belgium under what he called his "private estate" was the worst form of humanity, more remarkable than the holocaust by the Nazis.

The African blood was shed for military conflicts such as the two world wars, and when the dust settled, a generation of pan-Africanists rose from the ashes. Leaders such as Kwame Nkrumah, sekou toure, Patrice Lumumba, Julius Nyerere, Kenneth Kaunda, etc., fought for freedom from colonialism and became fathers of great independent African states.

Africa is a great continent with a vast wealth of opportunity. 7 of the 25 fastest-growing economies in 2020 are based in Africa well, as the vibrancy of the growing young population on the continent provides the continent with a vast opportunity for innovation, a skillset, and a large growing market for economic development.

LEADERSHIP

Leadership? What is it, and how does it impact native Africans' and the continent's daily lives? Let's look at a definition of leadership from Wikipedia: a person, group, or organisation can "lead", influence, or direct other people, groups of people, or entire organisations. Leadership is both a research topic and a practical talent. The term "leadership" is frequently seen as a contentious one. Expert literature disputes diverse points of view on the subject, occasionally contrasting Eastern and Western leadership styles as well as (within the West) North American versus European styles.

Leadership is described as "a process of social influence in which a person can enlist the aid and support of others in accomplishing a common and ethical task" in academic settings in the United States. Leadership can be defined as a meaningful power relationship in which the power of one party (the "leader") promotes movement/change in others (the "followers"). Some people oppose the more conventional managerial views of leadership, which portray it as something that one person possesses or owns because of their position or authority, and instead support the idea that leadership is complex and can be found in both formal and informal roles at all levels of institutions.

As stated clearly in the above definitions, a leader must be able to lead or bring their team organisation or country to a successful page or end to help grow their country's economy, interpersonal relationships, and many other things. Still, in most parts of the world, including Africa, we feel the brunt of lousy leadership endured by a whole race nation or even continent.

The world is at the peak of a severe economic crisis, and many blame the Russia-Ukraine war, but as an African, I beg to differ slightly. See, in Africa, politicians contest for power with pure intentions of bettering their nations, therefore, blasting their opponents, who are mostly those in power before them, and calling them all sorts of names after going through countless failed elections and losing most of their seed capital and investments into these campaigns and stuff, they tend to defile their virgin thoughts of building a corrupt free, dynamic and economically stable economy for their homeland to have this particular thought in their head, "Nnipa ebeye bi, wa menye ne nyinaa" Akan proverbs from the Ashanti's in Ghana which primarily transliterate to "A person came but to fulfil some and not all" and so go on on a rampage to ravage and plunder the country, the very thing they preached against. From these observations and being an African and a human of sound mind, I can boldly say that the woes of Africa as a whole are stemmed from lousy leadership practices originating from mentalities and percepts garnered over the years of toil. Let's consider the causes of terrible leadership practices ruining Africa.

CHAPTER 2

THE SPIRIT OF SACRIFICE

"Real leaders must be ready to sacrifice all for the freedom of their people, and what counts in life is not the mere fact that we have lived. It is what difference we have made to the lives of others that will determine the significance of the life we lead" (Nelson M. Speech, April 1998 Address by President Nelson Mandela at the opening of the Emthonjeni Youth Centre, Pretoria). Considering this quote from Nelson Mandela, whom most African Leaders claim to be their role model yet practice contrary to what he preaches, most of these leaders don't want to risk their lavish lifestyle or status to enable a "common" citizen to enjoy a better life, these include and not limited to considering hardships in certain given nations and yet Member of Parliaments are receiving exorbitant allowances and trips which can cater for entire communities for months. Sacrifice is one of the most incredible things in the world, but it seems most leaders have paid no heed to it; they don't seem to know about it or prefer to ignore it. Taking a country like Ghana as a case study, even with the rise in the price of gas, petrol, and diesel as well as electricity, top government officials enjoy fuel coupons and their electricity bills being taken off by the government; they call it "benefits of being in power", to add salt to injury, when a government official is moving around, he moves in a convoy of not less than five cars, and the same government fund is taking care of that expenditure. Leaders advise the country's citizens to report to their local health facilities, which are filled with experienced but unempathetic health personnel who, for about two working months, in a roll hasn't been paid, in a facility not adequately equipped with medical devices to aid in proper healthcare delivery and fly his family out to world-renowned health facilities abroad for the slightest headaches. This issue boils down to there not being any sacrifice in the hearts of the leaders.

FAVOURITISM

Have you ever been in a school Drama where you felt a specific lead role befits you or another person? Still, it was given out to an unqualified person because He knows the Drama director or is the ward of a member of the school board of directors? This example is one of the most frequent lousy leadership practices in Africa, occurring just about every single day, In stores, job interviews, schools, and even churches. Yes! Churches, the ones who frequently gift pastors, are the ones who are mostly attended to when they are in need; one can argue that it is because they gift the pastors or the leaders, but in a genuine sense, as a leader, you mustn't be biased. When hiring for jobs, most recruiters look for tribe members or clansmen even though they might be unqualified. They get hired and start looting or mismanaging state resources, which ruins the integrity of the department or ministry they are working with.

SOLUTIONS FOR BASIC PROBLEMS IN AFRICA

Africa has a diverse culture, abundant natural resources, and untapped human potential. Poverty, a lack of access to healthcare and other necessities like clean water, a lack of economic opportunity, political unrest, natural disasters, and the prevalence of deadly illnesses like HIV/AIDS, malaria, and tuberculosis are just a few of the pressing problems that Africa is currently dealing with.

These issues are interconnected and often reinforce each other, creating a cycle of poverty and underdevelopment. Addressing them requires a comprehensive approach that includes investment in infrastructure, education, and healthcare and promoting good governance and sustainable economic development.

Through trade alliances, research and development partnerships, and financial and technical help, the international community may support African countries' efforts to overcome their problems.

Despite its challenges, Africa has enormous potential for growth and development. Working together can help the continent and its people have a better future. Below is a summary of the problems in Africa, along with suggestions for remedies.

The lack of access to quality education is a significant issue in Africa, caused by inadequate infrastructure and resources, a shortage of qualified teachers, and poverty. Governments, international organisations, and NGOs must work together to address this issue to give students the tools and assistance they need to succeed.

Access to portable clean water is necessary for human survival, yet many African people lack access to it. The leading causes of the lack of access to clean water are poor infrastructure, inadequate water management, and environmental degradation. The consequences of this problem are severe, including the spread of water-borne diseases, time-consuming water collection tasks, and negative impacts on agriculture. Addressing this issue requires a comprehensive approach, including improving water infrastructure, investing in water management, and promoting environmental sustainability. Governments, international organisations, and NGOs must work together to provide clean water and ensure everyone can access this fundamental human right.

The lack of access to healthcare in Africa is a multifaceted issue caused by poor infrastructure, inadequate funding, and a shortage of trained medical personnel. This problem leads to a significant impact on public health and the economy. Addressing this issue requires a comprehensive approach, including investing in healthcare infrastructure, increasing funding for healthcare, and training and retaining medical personnel. Collaboration between governments, international organisations, and NGOs is essential to provide healthcare to those in need and ensure access to this fundamental human right.

The lack of access to necessities in Africa, such as food, water, shelter, and healthcare, is a significant problem caused by poverty, political instability, and environmental degradation. The severe consequences include malnutrition, poor health, and high mortality rates, particularly among children. This problem must be addressed holistically, addressing poverty, fostering sustainable development, and helping needy people. Governments, international organisations, and NGOs must cooperate to guarantee access to these fundamental human rights.

The lack of access to economic opportunities in Africa is caused by inadequate infrastructure, limited investment in education and training, and low levels of foreign investment. This problem results in poverty, unemployment, and underemployment. Addressing this issue requires a comprehensive approach that includes investing in education and training, promoting entrepreneurship, and increasing foreign investment. To ensure that everyone has access to economic opportunities and can contribute to Africa's economic growth and development, governments, international organisations, and NGOs must cooperate.

Africa has a serious issue with access to basic necessities due to poverty, poor infrastructure, and a lack of resources. With serious repercussions like starvation, ill health, and high death rates, this issue affects access to clean water, food, housing, and healthcare. A comprehensive strategy is necessary to address this issue, including enhancing infrastructure, increasing funding for programs that address fundamental requirements, and promoting sustainable development. Governments, international organisations, and NGOs must work together to provide access to these fundamental human rights and improve the quality of life for those in need.

Political instability is a significant issue in many African countries caused by various factors, including ethnic conflict and weak governance. It leads to corruption, violence, and a lack of funding for essential public services, resulting in poverty, poor economic growth, and human rights violations. Addressing political instability requires a comprehensive approach that promotes good governance, invests in education, and addresses the root causes of conflict. The international community can also support peacebuilding efforts and promote transparency and accountability in government.

Limited economic opportunities in Africa are a significant problem caused by a lack of infrastructure and investment to develop the continent's natural resources. The resulting factor creates poverty, unemployment, and corruption, making it difficult to attract foreign investment. Investment in vital infrastructure, assistance for small and medium-sized businesses, and global collaboration to promote economic growth are all necessary to address this issue.

Natural disasters in Africa are a significant issue as the continent is prone to droughts, floods, and other weather-related events that destroy crops, homes, and livelihoods, leading to poverty. Addressing this issue requires disaster preparedness, risk reduction, community resilience-building efforts, and international disaster response and recovery support.

Diseases such as HIV/AIDS, malaria, and tuberculosis significantly impact.

CHAPTER 3

CORRUPTION

"Leadership is neither easy nor fast nor without massive risks. Though the rewards of leadership are often sweet and exceedingly rare, the danger of deploying it without proper consideration is such that it might, quite literally, screw over this generation and the next and the one after it, too," begins Timehin Adegbeye, who is the editor of Chimurenga Chronic, a free, Pan-African journal. "And if we survive to see the day when there is no power on this land that has not been freely given to the people by their consent," she continues, "we will only have avoided an end we brought very close upon ourselves."

Adegbeye's essay addresses the selfishness of African leaders and, more broadly, selfishness in leadership. She argues that to be an effective leader, one must put the people above themselves. It's a perspective that drives at the heart of the leadership crisis in Africa, a problem, she says, that is characterised not just by corruption but by human nature.

What causes corruption is the main issue. Fundamentally, one's worldview will affect how one makes decisions as a leader and determine whether corruption is an "accepted practice." One's values, which define one's character, influence one's perspective. Building trust and a relationship with people being led that is service-oriented and empathic is the foundation of good leadership.

POOR ACCOUNTABILITY

A friend once commented that African Politicians act like Bollywood actors, I was disturbed when he made that comment, but he clarified further by showing me a video of a member of parliament in one Western African country feigning fainting to skip querying from a panel of a committee assigned to investigate purported misused funds of the state. This is the sad truth, lack of accountability.

THEORETICAL APPROACH TO PROBLEM-SOLVING

Ironically there is this saying that "Empty barrels make the most noise," the big act but no-show attitude of most African leaders is beyond disgusting; if most African leaders are tasked to deliver a solution to a problem, they immerse themselves solely in the theatrics to please the populace of the country to gain favour, and if in case they do so indeed, they make a mess out of it without considering certain vital aspects of the solution to be made, they use archaic methods to solve modern problems.

SELFISH DECISIONS

Opinion: A politician might have his eyes on the next election instead of the generation to come; a religious leader can be channelling all their energies to securing themselves a comfortable life or living ostentatiously and creating a monopoly for themselves; a head of state might be thinking about protecting his ill-gotten wealth instead of offering protection to his citizens, and ensuring that the plight of the majority attracts adequate attention from the powers that be. Once again, Africans have suffered terribly and continued to care for some of these short-sighted "leaders."

CURBING BAD LEADERSHIP

True leaders always practice the 3Rs: Self-respect, Respect for others and Responsibility for all their actions (The Dalai Lama [Tenzon Gyatso], 2016). Suppose ethical leaders possess a strong sense of integrity, humility, and respect for the people who elect them to positions of authority. In that case, there are no boundaries to what they can accomplish.

In his presentation to the United Nations General Assembly on April 10, 1984, Thomas Sankara, a great African leader who personified what a nation aspires for in a political leader, used the following remarks that should be more relevant than ever to Africans today:

"We have chosen a different path to achieve better results. We have chosen to establish new techniques. We have decided to seek forms of organisation that are better adapted to our civilisation, abruptly and once and for all rejecting all kinds of external diktats so that we can create the conditions for dignity in keeping with our ambitions. We refuse simple survival. We want to ease pressures, to free our countryside from medieval stagnation or regression. We want to democratise our society and open our minds to a universe of collective Responsibility so that we may be bold enough to invent the future." (United Nations, 1984).

NEGOTIATION

Is there a way to rearrange basic fabrics that support life or revise systems in the aspects of trading our natural blessings constructively for a needful long-term commodity to make life more enjoyable in Africa? By nature, humans and animals find themselves in an environment that is relatively spacious enough to accommodate each other but calls for the survival of the fittest due to limited resources. Naturally, conspecifics compete over limited resources, such as territories, food, etc., by fighting or communication. Such a communication process may involve negotiation to rule out their differences and ensure everyone is satisfied. Considering how ants, common insects of the family Formicidae with a population of about 20 quadrillion on earth, stockpile food, critical observation shows that, during the dry season, ants embark on a mission to store their food to survive during the rainy season. In the process, hundreds of ants line up linearly and communicate among themselves as the ant at the anterior end of the queue collects the food and passes it on to the next and so on until it reaches the last ant at the posterior end of the line up continuously and repeatedly until they accumulate enough food. This form of communication and unity to undertake such a course is a form of negotiation. Practically wherever there are limited resources to compete, the possible options for the parties involved are slavery, tyranny, or negotiation. Especially if there are no rules or traditions to control one who yearns to be the oppressor, negotiation becomes the saviour to enhance peace after the parties' preferences are satisfied fairly or understandably.

What is negotiation? Life is all about negotiation. Everything one does daily is negotiation, even though most of such do not seem obvious and hence one may not realise. People constantly negotiate their way through life. For example, one with lovers or allies continuously negotiates to prove oneself worthy of whatever benefits one receives. Negotiation, which is not apparent to realise, is because one does it subconsciously. Consider a boss treating his workers well and motivating them to work productively as a form of negotiation; a mother singing for a baby to make the child smile instead of crying and giving food to her hungry pet to stop it from barking or meowing are all forms of negotiation. Coincidentally, life has made everyone a negotiator by default. According to "Getting to Yes: Negotiating

Agreement Without Giving In", the author writes ", Like it or not, you are a negotiator…Everyone negotiates something every day" (Roger F, William U. and Bruce P., 2011). Delving into the diverse definitions of negotiation is punctuated by the discussion below.

According to the author of Getting to Yes, negotiating is a "back-and-forth communication designed to reach an agreement when you and the other side have some interests that are shared and others that are opposed." (Roger Fisher, William Ury and Bruce Patton, 2011). In other words, the author of Negotiation and Aristotles Rhetoric: Truth over Interests? Alexios Arvanitis from the University of Crete and Karampatzos Antonis from the National and Kapodistrian University of Athens write in their psychology article, "That negotiation is typically regarded as the parties' effort to achieve a favourable outcome and thus, win-win outcomes have become the ultimate prescriptive desideratum of negotiation." (Arvanitis, Alexios & Antonis, Karampatzos. 2011). Similarly, in The Mind and Heart of the Negotiator, experts like Leigh Thompson define negotiation as "an interpersonal decision-making process that is necessary whenever we cannot achieve our objectives single-handedly". (Thompson, Leigh, 2005).

Simplifying the above, in their book Judgement in Managerial Decision Making, Max H. Bazerman and Don A. Moore write, "When two or more parties need to reach a joint decision but have different preferences, they negotiate" (Max H. Bazerman and Don A. Moore. 2012). The central goal of negotiation is thus to limit combativeness, which may lead to chaos or catastrophe. For example, one must lay out the problem's space hypothesis when deciding on a complicated issue or situation. In other words, one should be able to provide answers to possible worse scenarios if the needful is not done to be able to specify in a bracket a discussion of what might be going on. Even though it's complex to arrive at the best decision because, in the problem space hypothesis, one should be able to divide oneself into two states of mind, whereby the first virtual being stands for tackling to solve the issue, and the other also react proactively by means possible to complicate the decision making or to yield poor decision whereby both virtual beings act impartially, critically and seems realistically simultaneously in one's mind. As Prof. Jordan Peterson says, "It's hard to negotiate because you have to suspend your judgement and have a symbolic war that doesn't erupt into a real war, and you have to solve it, and people have to enact with your solution." Again, a good decision will be made if one constructively scrutinises the situation and establishes a distinction between the hypothesis and the reality description.

Additionally, just as negotiation happens in numerous aspects of life, it also happens in political, diplomatic, and international relations. The creation of international organisations, regimes, and a set of international laws and rules has greatly increased the effectiveness of international negotiations. This explains why peaceful interactions and communication are considerably more commonplace now than in the past. As a vital instrument in international relations between countries and international organisations, negotiation is best described as Diplomatic Negotiation. Despite the challenges associated with negotiation, as discussed in the write-up, most African diplomats who negotiate on behalf of their countries are well-trained. Hence, they understand the dynamics, protocols, rules, elements, and stages of diplomatic negotiation; and the tension surrounding the negotiation table. In that sense, it raises eyebrows on the African land when outcomes from negotiations with foreign counterparts end up enslaving the Africans instead of liberation.

The parties' desire to understand the process and offer suggestions for potential outcomes, i.e., outcomes that serve the interests of all the negotiating parties, is what makes negotiations most important. Given that win-win outcomes are the ultimate goal of any negotiation, why is Africa still dissatisfied with the outcomes of negotiations on our natural resources and other diplomatic issues? Could it be that our Diplomats do not negotiate well? Do they negotiate for themselves and forget about who they represent? Or, they lose because they cannot open up their space of available options on the international negotiation table? Conversely, as Prof. Jordan Peterson says, you can't negotiate with anyone unless you can say no; you can't say no unless you set yourself up with alternatives. The begged questions lead to the below discussion concerning how African leaders negotiate on diplomatic grounds at the expense of the continent (Africa).

HOW AFRICA LEADERS NEGOTIATE WITH FOREIGN COUNTERPARTS AT THE EXPENSE OF THE CONTINENT(AFRICA)

Africa must continue participating in international trade discussions as it is being squeezed. Without creating new opportunities for new products or markets, policy changes in its markets, which supporters wrongly refer to as "liberalisation," quickly diminish the competitive advantage granted to traditional exporters to established markets. The foregoing introduction analyses how the World Trade Organization (WTO) and the bilateral trade agreements of the Quad (Canada, the EU, Japan, and the USA) have changed. It pays particular attention to the Common Agricultural Policy (CAP) adjustments and the Economic Partnership Agreements (EPAs) that sub-Saharan Africa must negotiate with the EU.

African trade negotiators have recently "punched above their weight," which was necessary given how quickly trade patterns are changing. The products that are exported, imported, and consumed locally are changing, all to the detriment of Africa. Its position as a preferred beneficiary of trade preferences in some markets (but not in others) is deteriorating quickly. Its terms of access to non-regional markets will increasingly be the same as those of its rivals. As a result, trade authorities are now focusing more on Geneva than on Brussels. However, as the stalled Doha process attests, the international system is still seen as being inadequately sensitive to Africa's demands. In the meantime, some of the region's long-standing trading partners are requesting reverse privileges under the pretext of free trade agreements (FTAs). Although they are positioned as promoting regional integration and the multilateral system, it is uncertain whether the outcome will be beneficial.

The region has been exposed to Africa's vulnerability in terms of its capacity to strategise and negotiate as a result of this newly discovered volatility in the region's international economic ties. The World Trade Organization (WTO) agenda is only the tip of an iceberg, including numerous overlapping trade negotiations. The issues faced by overworked (or nonexistent) diplomatic missions in Geneva to deal with it have received considerable media attention. The demands for a clear line of communication from economic stakeholders through line ministries to trade negotiators grow increasingly pronounced when existing connections become strained, and new ones need to be established. And the contrast between the ideal and the real world grows even more pronounced. Despite these drawbacks, African states have managed to participate in a wide variety of agreements, both inside and outside their own continent. Trade integration is already taking place within the Union Economique et Monétaire Ouest Africaine (UEMOA), the Common Market for Eastern and Southern Africa (COMESA), and the Southern African Development Community (SADC). The WTO has seen significant involvement from Africa. Additionally, talks with the European Union (EU) are underway to replace the current trading system.

One area where Africa has fought above its weight is the Doha Round. Before July 2002, the Africa Group provided more than one-third of the systemic cross-cutting issue suggestions and over two-thirds of all the specific submissions to the Committee on Trade and Development (CTD) (WTO, 2002: Annexes 2 and 3). African nations were also heavily represented at the Cancun Ministerial and in the complex WTO negotiations. However, the incident also highlighted the disparity of power inside the WTO. In situations when other members are not actively supportive, groups with superior numerical strength have more power to prevent mould than superior economic and technical strength. They can stop the adoption of proposals of which they disapprove significantly on principle, as was most clearly shown in Cancun. However, they are unable to compel other nations to adopt their demands. The WTO can only advance in a favourable direction if other members are willing to adapt the technical details of proposals as they develop to address African concerns. Despite the claims made in the Doha Declaration, several important WTO members have been less than accommodating to the demands the Africa Group believes they have. This is one of the issues the Africa Group is facing. The contentious discussions around special and differential treatment (SDT) highlight a larger issue that led to the failure in Cancun and the lack of significant advancement since then. The WTO's evolution as the keeper of trade rules pertinent to the fast-changing reality of global trade may depend on resolving these issues, making it challenging for Africa and the entire multilateral system. Both in theory and in fact, the WTO negotiation process does not automatically produce conclusions that are favourable to development. The General Agreement on Tariffs and Trade (GATT) negotiations were frequently tough-minded, with negotiators pursuing constrained, mercantilist objectives. According to the evidence from Doha thus far, the negotiating philosophy of mercantilism has not altered, and the commitment to stronger SDT has not yet been put into action.

This has raised concerns among many developing nations, not just those in Africa, as the transition from the GATT to the WTO has greatly increased the significance of "formal SDT." Numerous members benefited from the GATT's significant use of the potential for distinctive differentiation. This 'informal' SDT was made possible by including ambiguous language that may be interpreted differently by each GATT member in the papers. As a result, nations with differing ideas about what needs to be done can sign up to the same set of terms, certain that, after the ink is dry, they can be applied however they see fit. This escape route was eliminated by the Uruguay Round's novel idea of making dispute resolution binding. It's possible that, as a result, the WTO has evolved. The WTO's dispute settlement process has long focused on policies. Additionally, the percentage of cases brought by industrialised nations against developing nations has increased. A review of cases filed between 1995 and 2000 revealed a threefold increase in this percentage when compared to the GATT period (Delich, 2002: 76). The WTO's reputation is significantly more contentious than the GATT's, which is a corollary.

Many participants and observers view The SDT added to the documents for the Uruguay Round as inadequate. SDTs that are legally enforceable are absent from a large chunk of trade policy, and those that do exist are depleting assets. These two problems are the key ones. The first is especially harsh in the "new areas" of trade policy (such as services, government contracts, trade-related aspects of intellectual property rights (TRIPs), and competition policy) because there is no effective SDT, and it is frequently incredibly unclear what form more stringent restrictions will take. The vitality of commitments modulated by enforceable SDT will drop directly (if they are time-limited) and indirectly (if they involve decreasing obstacles that all members are gradually lowering) over time. Each of the three key components of SDT—modulation of promises, trade preferences, and expressions of support—displays these undesirable status quo characteristics. The most important SDT provision is the modification of obligations. For instance, the Agreement on Agriculture mandates that industrialised nations lower their tariffs by 36% over six years. However, developing nations only need to reduce their tariffs by 24% over ten years, and least developed nations are exempt from this requirement. It often satisfies the very minimum standard for effective SDT in that it is "legally enforceable": a WTO member may use the dispensations granted under SDT in its defence if another WTO member disputes its trade policies on the grounds that they are in violation of the Uruguay Round obligations. Consequently, India would have a strong defence in dispute resolution by pointing out that it only needed to liberalise by 24% if it were challenged because it has not decreased its agricultural tariffs by 36%. The 1979 Enabling Clause justifies the provision of greater market access via trade preferences (mostly by industrialised countries to developing and least developed countries). The expansion does not mandate that industrialised nations discriminate in favour of developing nations but allows them to do so. Market access could be offered for SDT in a variety of areas, but industrialised nations do not do this;

instead, they focus their limitations on developing nations. One example is the abuse of anti-dumping procedures. The Organisation for Economic Co-operation and Development (OECD) states are frequently accused of asserting that dumping has occurred when it is simply a case that developing countries are more competitive than domestic suppliers. This is far from using the provisions that exist within the WTO sensitively to reduce the disruption to developing country trade. The WTO status quo offers significant potential for SDT in the industrialised countries' cause, as in so many other instances, but only modest prospects in the cause of the poor countries! The latest disagreement between India and the EU has made it clear how far the provisions on trade preferences comply with the need for legal enforceability. The WTO's decision in the EU-India dispute opened the door for the EU to grant significant preferences to a recognisable group of nations dealing with comparable objective circumstances. A new Generalised System of Preferences (GSP), agreed in June 2005, was the EU's response. The main innovation in the new GSP is a special trade regime, to be called GSP+, that will be available to many developing countries (but not all of the poorest) and improve access to the EU (though not as well as is available to the African, Caribbean, and Pacific (ACP) countries (under Cotonou) or to least developed countries (LDCs) under "Everything But Arms" - EBA). A nation must ratify and successfully implement the 16 main United Nations/International Labour Organization treaties on human and labour rights and at least seven (of the 11) environmental and governance issues conventions. Additionally, nations must adhere to "vulnerability" standards based on the value of their exports. Even if they may be inferior, larger nations and those with a wider variety of exports are more likely to fail the vulnerability test. The GSP+ may radically alter the balance of benefits and drawbacks for sub-Saharan Africa (SSA) of economic partnership agreements (EPAs) with the EU if it avoids the WTO challenge, as shown below. On the one hand, if GSP+ is widely adopted, SSA preferences in the EU will be severely undermined. On the other hand, it gives SSA states an option to EPAs, which offers many states' current exports a similar amount of strong market access. The Uruguay Round texts are littered with several statements of support for developing nations, which make up the third area of SDT, which is completely unenforceable. For instance, the General Agreement on Trade in Services (GATS) Article 4 talks about encouraging developing nations to participate more in global services trade through "negotiated specific commitments relating to the strengthening of their domestic services capacity, improving their access to distribution channels and liberalising market access in sectors and modes of supply of export interest to them. Similar provisions are included about the requirements of emerging nations that net import food. A developing country that feels wronged cannot compel another member (or an international organisation) to act in a way that it deems consistent with these undertakings, either inside or outside the WTO. Unhappiness that they were 'hoodwinked' into signing the Single Undertaking of the Uruguay Round by promises that were, literally, not worth the paper they were written on, stems from a significant portion of the discontent expressed by developing countries in the WTO about the failures of SDT. The SDT provisions need to be made somewhat enforceable as part of the Doha discussions, or existing rules need to be changed (or future rules tailored) to take into account the SDT provisions' non-enforceability. Because the SDT provisions now in place are insufficient, the Doha Declaration made a commitment to strengthening and improving them. There is a deadlock because it has shown to be impossible for WTO members to put this pledge into real practice. Dealing with the flaws in the status quo is primarily a political issue rather than a technical one. Therefore, for any development provisions to be effective, they must be enforceable in the WTO. Even at this early stage of the talks, finding the flexibility to address important issues is still possible. However, given the lack of precise texts for the new rules, they must be stated in very general terms. Additionally, industrialised nations do not want to accept stringent, enforceable restrictions. If broad provisions are problematic now, how about more precise provisions later on when this is possible because draft texts can be changed? Suppose the Doha Round proceeds similarly to its predecessor, which is expected given that it seems to be an inherent challenge when discussing a large variety of complicated provisions simultaneously. In that case, the problem will likely be the dynamic of the discussions. There cannot be an agreement until the major WTO members have reached compromises. There is a compelling need to close the sale as soon as possible to avoid upsetting the consensus they can live with. Given that, after WTO agreements have been signed, whatever flaws are later revealed, it is practically impossible to modify them, the TRIPs Agreement is a standing warning of the danger of not incorporating binding SDT at an early stage of discussions. Many have questioned its suitability for developmental purposes, including the International Commission on Intellectual Property Rights (CIPR), founded by Clare Short, the former UK Secretary of State for Development, and whose secretariat is primarily staffed by employees of the UK Department for International Development. Its report raises questions about the necessity of establishing strict deadlines for developing nations to adopt international property (IP) rules as well as the viability of amending the agreement to do away with them (CIPR, 2002:160–161). The projected effects of international liberalisation on Africa's preferential trading arrangement with the EU, its largest market, will determine how the continent feels about it. There have been discussions about the relative virtues of multilateralism and regionalism, and there are benefits and drawbacks to moving fundamentally from the status quo to a far more liberal global trading regime. The relative attractions are significantly influenced by the period under consideration and the relevant socioeconomic actors. However, there may be indirect connections between this intellectual discussion and the problems up for the Doha Round.

The worst-case scenario for Africa is one in which the region experiences few, if any, identified gains from global free trade (due to the WTO's limited reform) but loses significant benefits under the current preferential regime. The Agreement on Agriculture hasn't undergone many extensive revisions to date, but the portents that have emerged thus far are worrying. This worst-case scenario might come to pass. In that situation, developments in the multilateral and preferential arena would be the cause of this. Since the crucial non-agricultural preference for clothes is already eroding, agriculture is the multilateral issue of greatest relevance. However, there are still some very strong preferences regarding temperate agriculture. But any combination of the following three types of change has the potential to undermine them:

• substantial international deregulation to lower OECD market access restrictions on agricultural imports; independent OECD state actions that impact lowering the returns to alterations to the preferential trade agreements; and preferential exporters.

Substantial liberalisation is the most significant modification to the WTO Agreement on Agriculture that could influence African preferences. As the opposite of protectionism, preferences are. By definition, a nation with a liberal trade policy is unable to grant some suppliers privileged access. The option of lowering these barriers to some extent for preferred trade partners only arises if it significantly restricts imports. The requirement of a pre-existing restriction is comfortably met by OECD market access barriers for agriculture: no less than 19 of the 33 HS chapters covered (in whole or in part) by the Agreement on Agriculture experience tariff peaks in at least one (and typically two or three) of the Quad states. According to what is known so far from Doha, even a successful end to the Round will leave most of these peaks in place. Peaks are significant because they indicate that even after significant reductions in tariffs, import barriers could remain high enough to prevent imports from reaching adequate levels. How likely is it that the Doha Round would lower tariff peaks to a point where significant imports are economically feasible? The problem that has emerged as one of the roadblocks to advancement is the one raised above. At the WTO ministerial in July 2005, the EU and others failed to agree on a negotiation strategy to eliminate the majority of extremely high peaks. Will there be a significant reduction in subsidies if there isn't a significant liberalisation? The tables of tariff peaks do not include cotton, the Cancun centre of attention for African issues. Because domestic US subsidies, not the Quad's market access restrictions, are the main issue with the Agreement on Agriculture for African cotton growers. 'Cotton, neither carded nor combed' (HS 520100) accounted for the majority of West Africa's cotton exports to the EU in 2002. Items under this HS subhead are subject to 0% MFN duties in the EU, Canada, and Japan. Although they are subject to a duty of up to 31.4 cents/kg in the USA, this is only equivalent to roughly 10% ad valorem. A major topic of discussion at Cancun was the difficulties that US subsidies to American cotton producers caused for West African cotton exporters. An Overseas Development

Institute (ODI) study contends that EU subsidies may also be detrimental to West and Central Africa because EU cotton production competes with developing countries' cotton production in third-country markets (ODI, 2004). Many critics pointed to the US offer on cotton as inadequate as a major reason negotiations were stalled. At the time this article was written, the problem was still open. Africa as a region is also interested in any rule changes that would tend to increase import costs and, as a result, result in a deterioration in their terms of trade because they are significant net importers of grains. Imports have become more and more important to the area. Contrary to what some people believe, food aid, which has made up a relatively modest (and reduced in the final decade covered) percentage of the total, has not been the main cause. Agricultural exports, likewise impacted by WTO regulations (notably those on preferences), provide a sizeable portion of the foreign money used to pay for imports. Therefore, any change in either side of the trade equation could indirectly impact people's access to food by changing the total amount of food accessible in a nation or how it is distributed among the various food categories (over which people have varying entitlements). Preferential and regional trade agreements with specific trading partners will inevitably continue to play a significant role in Africa's trade profile, given the Doha Round's poor development, at least in agriculture. However, a shift is taking place that might drastically alter the region's benefits historically reaped from these partnerships. The EU is by far Africa's largest market, importing over 50% more goods than the other three Quad states. Not many goods are imported into the EU but into one of the other three Quad members. At least 1,692 of the 1,710 African imports the EU made in 2000 with a value of $1 million or more were covered by a preference for at least one exporter from the continent. Only 491 of the items were imported into the

USA, the second-largest Quad importer, and half of those items qualified for preferences. There are eight trade agreements between Africa and the EU. For the GSP, all African nations are qualified. The Cotonou trade policy and, in the case of the least developed countries, the "Everything but Arms" (EBA) rule both benefit those who live south of the Sahara (except for South Africa). Furthermore, bilateral agreements exist between South Africa and most North African nations. These agreements, which have been in place for a while but are currently being converted into reciprocal FTAs with many of the same terms, apply to the countries of North Africa. The Barcelona Declaration's goal of establishing a Euro-Mediterranean free trade area by 2010 inside the GSP framework, which provides wider and deeper preferences, serves as a concrete illustration. The GSP is a fundamental component in the USA's situation. However, for 125 of the 491 goods (or 26% of all imports into the USA from Africa), AGOA offers the most advantageous treatment within the GSP framework. At the same time, more imported goods are subject to zero MFN levies in nations outside of the EU. In the EU, the percentage is slightly over one-quarter, despite the fact that, in absolute terms, the EU offers a 0% MFN on more items than all three other countries. The proportion ranges from almost two-thirds for Canada to just over half for Japan and 42% for the USA. The two pieces of data are connected. Due to the fact that it imposes zero MFN duties on the majority of its imports from Africa, Canada is unable to provide preferences. Preferences are the antithesis of protectionism, as previously stated. Liberal-trade economists typically favour multilateral liberalisation over preferences for the reasons mentioned above. Additionally, there is the political opinion that to borrow from Bhagwati's famous adage, the entrenched interests produced by preferences may act as a "stumbling block" rather than a "building block" for multilateralism. But regionalism might be the second-best option in situations like the current one, where multilateral liberalisation is not an option (since there is no agreement in the WTO). The GSP is the cornerstone of Japan's and Canada's preferential trade agreements with Africa. Both offer unique conditions for the least developed nations.

Although the implications of reciprocity have received most of the attention from ACP interests, the negotiations must address several other crucial problems. These all revolve around the idea that the current trade regime needs to be restored since it is deteriorating quickly. The ACP must take the initiative to state their expectations because the EU's mandate makes no explicit recommendations for enhancing its import policy and just agrees to comply with ACP requests in some areas. In order to achieve the goals mentioned above, research will be necessary to develop these activities. The ACP Guidelines clearly mention the necessity of evaluating the effects of CAP reform.

Additionally, the EU's positions in the WTO must be considered (and attempted to influence) in the ACP's demands for treating its agricultural exports under EPAs. It appears quite likely that the ongoing discussions about the Agreement on Agriculture will not lead to a significantly more lenient EU import policy for goods covered by the CAP. As a result, there will always be a chance for strong ACP preferences. Ensuring this potential is realised will be the goal of the negotiation process.

Initial study on those products now covered by tariff-rate quotas (TRQs) is given high priority given that the EU has recommended in its mandate to eliminate all quantitative limits. These include steak, rice, and sugar. In order to help formulate a bargaining position that meets the interests of all ACP countries, early research should determine the effects on ACP exporters of eliminating any quantitative constraints on their exports to the EU. The rules of origin and market access for agricultural products are the two crucial improvements that must be made. The idea to expand EBA coverage to all ACP states was included in the initial draft of the Commission's mandate but was later abandoned due to internal disagreements. Reviving it is necessary, as is including it in the Euro-Med Agreements with North Africa. In addition to eliminating all export restrictions currently in place, this would ease tension between the least developed nations and the others in regional accords for Africa. The experience with AGOA and its lax restrictions on using imported components to produce apparel for less developed nations proves that the Cotonou standards are unrealistic regarding origin. Regulations governing cumulation need to be more lenient, and the amount of processing necessary needs to be decreased. The suggestion to incorporate a services component in EPAs is possibly the most exciting aspect for Africa. SSA must choose whether to enthusiastically use this chance to secure better terms for its services exports or to play defence against domestic providers. However, in either scenario, all governments will need to understand better what may be at stake. Barriers abound in the global exchange of services. While there have been significant reductions in trade barriers for products over the past 50 years, several laws and other restrictions still apply to the international trade of services. These critters frequently erect complicated, indirect, and opaque barriers, which can be barely noticeable until someone tries to export.

The world of trade policy is rapidly evolving in ways that significantly impact Africa's ability to compete. The process of adjustment, which may be significant and require change over a lengthy period in many economic and institutional domains, is one activity that involves determining which changes are unavoidable and starting the adjustment process. Another is trying to steer the policy discussion in less harmful ways whenever possible. Although the focus of this working paper has been on demonstrating the modifications and recommendations for the second task, the urgency and importance of the first task have not been diminished. One key finding is that Africa should question the economic explanations offered by those who support the most harmful policies. These are sometimes justified on the grounds that they represent a step toward liberalisation, which would eventually improve global welfare, and that Africa must "stop living in the past and accept change." Based on what is currently known, there is little reason to believe that CAP reform or EPAs will directly result in any global welfare increases. They will surely result in adjustment costs for Africa.

Furthermore, it is untrue that "trade preferences have seen their day," as the advocates of these measures assert. What is real is that many current preferences are vanishing quickly. However, there are many opportunities to replace them with new preferences because one of the two objective requirements remains true: the OECD states are still very protectionist in some trade areas in commodities and services. The second prerequisite—political will on the part of some OECD nations to grant Africa greater open access to these markets—appears to be missing. Even for LDCs, tight rules of origin are used to temper liberal access policies like EBA. Africa can thus argue its point forcefully without appearing to disagree with the general consensus regarding the merits of a liberal international trade policy.

Additionally, it is a flag under which it can carry on contributing actively to the development of global trade policy. But there are two distinct difficulties. The difficulty is in addressing the first barrier, which is easily understood. The issue is that these discussions lay a heavy burden on society. It is frequently observed that, compared to African governments, the negotiation teams of the larger OECD nations are massive. However, it's important to keep in mind that the gap in size also indicates a variation in composition. OECD delegates represent producer and consumer interests. They are responsible for determining the proposed rules' potential economic effects before drafting recommendations for the rules that would have the greatest economic benefits. Additionally, the entire delegation works in a setting where civil society organisations evaluate and advocate for national policies that consider various socioeconomic groups' concerns. In this sense, the frequently reported issue of understaffing in many African missions in Geneva (mind alone Brussels, Washington, and Tokyo) slightly misses the mark. Or else, it's only the proverbial "tip of the iceberg." Even more significant is the absence of a comprehensive structure that connects trade negotiators with producer and consumer organisations within a nation and can define society's offensive and defensive interests in every given set of discussions. Even with a full staff, the Geneva delegations operate in a vacuum without this.

The second difficulty is less widely acknowledged. It is that the market always has a propensity to move more quickly than the authorities, and globalisation may be causing this gap to grow. Therefore, it is not a given that the status quo will continue to apply if rules are not changed. It could imply that the market is allowed a more free hand de facto, if not de jure, and that the old rulebook becomes progressively outdated as it fails to handle new trading practices. The linked issue is that the multilateral system's impasse may lead to like-minded nations creating their own sub-multilateral regulations regardless of their source. While these wouldn't apply de facto to people who aren't partners, there is a chance that they might. Africa already feels the effects of completely unconstitutional agricultural standards set by European retailers that are unassailable. Bring things under some sort of public authority in order to prevent the scope of private rule-making from spiralling out of hand. Africa's issue is to avoid the possibility that, in the absence of public regulation, the private sector would set the game's rules and the twin challenges of inappropriacy of new public laws (multilateral or regional). The area cannot be taken for granted in international trade negotiations, as its negotiators have shown to the rest of the world in recent years. The challenge from now on is to build the capacity to create more proactive, constructive rule modifications that will better meet Africa's unique demands.

HOW THE INFERIORITY COMPLEX IS AFFECTING THE GROWTH OF AFRICA AND HOW TO SOLVE IT FOR AFRICA DEVELOPMENT

The phrase "inferiority complex" is typically used to refer to persistent feelings of inadequacy and insecurity. People with an inferiority complex may struggle with constant self-doubt, low self-esteem, and a desire to avoid social situations. The 'white is right' mentality is ingrained in many Africans, which has had detrimental impacts on our cultures. The confession of a Frenchman travelling in West Africa was posted on Instagram. The man, Jean Michel, asserts to have had over 600 pregnancies after sleeping with over 1,400 girls. How was this possible? Because Michel was wealthy and white, the women would swarm around him. When you hear "The Western World," what comes to mind? North America and Western Europe? Powerful? Organised? Richer? Educated? Better? Initial thoughts are far more optimistic. The issue is that billions of people have idolised the Western World as an ideal place, especially those who do not live there. The rose-coloured lens through which we view the West is an altered viewpoint that needs to be corrected. During the slave trade, Africans began to feel inferior to individuals with lighter skin tones. While our people suffered, white folks lived luxurious lives as the oppressors. It spread the belief "white is right." Africans started to imitate Western culture to escape the sufferings imposed upon them. Even though something isn't incorrect in and of itself, the problem is how it's thought of and the extreme steps it leads our people to adopt. This "white is right/better" mentality allowed Michel to attract so many ladies and have the guts to announce his intention to go on another sex tour. We have been brainwashed to respect foreigners and trash our own. Why do businesses prefer to recruit foreigners over locals? Why do we think that "expats" have it better than us? Why do we take them at their word and be forgiving, but we are rude to our blood who are in a similar situation or worse off than we are? Although not all Africans have this mindset, what should we do about the millions who do? Most people believe everyone else is superior to us because of our perceived African inferiority. When he stated it five years ago, a man in Accra almost hurt my ribs from laughing so hard: "If God had given Black ladies beards, they would put extensions to them."

He was serious, after all. "Look at the Black woman of today," he added. She adds extensions to her hair for decoration. She uses extensions to fill in her brows. She has extensions for both her fingernails and toenails. Thank God He did not give them beards. Additionally, they would have expanded them. An awful Black woman. The man argued that African/Black people have what is known as an "inferiority complex," which causes us to reject who we are and our God-given gifts in favour of emulating those of others. As a result, we feel less than human if we don't act like Europeans. Everything in Europe or America has to be superior to ours. To seem aristocratic, we choose European names for our first names. If not, we believe we are doomed. Or we may feel underdressed if we don't wear a suit and tie like the Europeans. Suit and tie attire have largely replaced other traditional clothing in Southern Africa, giving people there an exaggerated sense of their significance. And whether you're a government or even private sector official, woe is you if you don't dress that way. And despite the day's sweltering heat, tragedy will still befall you. Imagine that you must still wear a suit and tie in Africa's notoriously hot 30- to 35-degree climate to feel important and be taken seriously in the workplace. In some African nations, observing the President in his office without a suit and tie is illegal. Imagine that an African is prohibited from visiting his elected President in the State House without donning European clothing. I think it's pure folly. However, It is not practised by European settlers in Southern Africa, who ought to make a fetish of donning a suit and tie. They enjoy the fresh air while wearing their unadorned shirts and shorts. It is not practised by European settlers in Southern Africa, who ought to make a fetish of donning a suit and tie. They enjoy the fresh air while wearing their unadorned shirts and shorts. They work tirelessly on their vast farms while wearing hats or caps; at the end of the year, they have millions of dollars. The African covers himself in a coat and tie, ignores the importance of fresh air, favours writing instruments, and ends the year with almost little savings. It makes sense that our ladies have evolved into walking extensions. The Beautiful Ones Are Not Yet Born, a 1968 publication by Ghanaian novelist and Egyptologist Ayi Kwei Armah, stated: "There is something so horrible in observing a black man straining at all times to impersonate the dark ghost of a European... If his white master denies him any, the black man who has spent his entire life trying to escape into Whiteness has no power. The notion that Africans are subhuman compared to other races, especially Caucasians and that we must imitate their behaviours to feel human is a fabrication unsupported by historical evidence. We are aware that throughout the time of the slave trade and when they physically colonised Africa and exercised control over us, the Europeans imposed that idea on the African people. But the Europeans still lived in caves and had no idea what a window was when our African predecessors had created important civilisations and pyramids (the equivalent of today's skyscrapers), notably in Ancient Egypt! Muslims from West and Northwest Africa who had converted to Islam crossed the Mediterranean Sea to colonise Spain, Portugal, Sicily, Crete, and southern France between 711 AD and 1492, a span of 781 years. They also introduced agriculture, medicine, civilisation, and general enlightenment to Europe. These Africans were referred to as Mauros by the Greeks and Romans; their names were Moro, Moir, and Mór in the Spanish, French, and Italian Romance languages. In England, they were referred to as Moors, in Germany as Mauren, and in the Netherlands as Moorrees. But they all referred to "black or dark people."(Ayi A. Kwei, 1968). And these Africans enlightened Europe by building magnificent towns and palaces in Spain and Portugal. As a result, European aristocratic society during the time they refer to as their "Dark Ages" immortalised the Moors on their emblems. The Moors invaded Spain and ruled Crete for 125 years and Sicily for more than 200 years. 729AD, they conquered southern France's Lyon, Macon, and Chalon-sur-Saone. In 846 AD, they besieged Rome. They gained Sicily from the Normans in 878, and 20 years later, after conquering Otto II of Germany, they took southern Italy. The Moors may have contributed the most to medieval Europe's educational system. Spain was overrun with several educational institutions that imparted the time's ideologies and sciences. History reveals that during the height of the Moorish Empire, Spain (also known as Al-Andalus by the Moors) drew intellectuals from far-flung Muslim regions and England, France, Germany and Italy. Native Americans in North America also created enormous stone monuments known as the Colossal Heads to commemorate the Africans who travelled from West Africa to South and Central America and influenced the cultures there. So, who claims that Africans are beneath anyone? Yes, other races have surpassed us in many areas of life since the collapse of the African civilisations. We are unable to contest such an assertion. But that doesn't mean we are beneath them. For millennia, we were the First World and the centre of the universe. It is a universal truth that as civilisations fall apart, the people who built them go astray, leaving other peoples or races to advance. But that in no way diminishes their worth in comparison to contemporary saints.

Socio-economics must consciously ascertain what is wrong with Africa's sense of standards and values because the inferiority complex is almost associated with the African nation. Anyone outside the continent finds it challenging to purchase African produce without concern conveniently. But in reality, it's not just because we are Africans that we have this terrible reputation; better yet, it's not like the black race is cursed. Our attitudes and self-perceptions have been impacted by how our race is associated with being inferior. We believe everything foreign is far superior to anything made or found on this continent. We accept foreign foods, entertainment, clothing, and even thoughts. We don't understand what happens in the creative and entrepreneurial industries. Africans love to absorb ideas and opinions from other continents and nations without considering whether they are practical in this particular sense. African customers' choices have frequently been constrained to inexpensive, subpar-quality, unbranded goods in several areas. About 80% of Nigerians who typically would consider purchasing a local brand are discouraged by the product's quality, how their friends and family might feel about it, or a lack of selection. Even in the algorithmic and high-speed trading age, Africa is off-limits. The lack of direct investment in Africa is primarily due to the outdated market infrastructure. Africa has not yet reached the point of appreciating its native produce or content, as mentioned. It's horrible that we continue to believe that everything made on this continent must somehow be inferior. However, if Africa is to prosper, it must shift from being a consuming continent to one that produces goods and services of the highest calibre. These standards would be welcomed elsewhere in the globe. Almost every African country export raw material to the rest of the world, but acquiring finished commodities based on technology is still exceedingly difficult. It is impossible to overstate the successes of African music and entertainment, and it is because of this that we need to focus on other areas of our economy. We must embrace a particular lifestyle to maintain excellence in every aspect of our lives as producers. Similar to other countries of the world, Africa has talented individuals who make a wide variety of scientific discoveries. The best of these abilities come from humble or even lower social groups, which is essential to note. How come? In the end, only providence can tell us! And perhaps destiny will decree that these abilities have to discover ways to end poverty despite living in substandard or modest circumstances. The above-said talented African individuals make every effort to find the finest answers to the issues they deal with daily since they face particular challenges in their environment for which the solutions they have discovered could, in an ideal world, aid in advancing their nation. Let's attempt to visualise this situation. Consider a young, brilliant African under 20 years who has created something innovative, like a generator that works on oxygen from the air or salted water instead of fuel. What if these inventors and innovators have demonstrated the viability of their technology through the construction of prototypes using scraps and other locally accessible materials? Well, they won't generally be taken seriously in Africa, yet at the same time, energy is a rare resource there. Herein lies the paradox: there are locally appropriate solutions to power Africa, yet decision-makers do not consider them. But how can this continent advance if we think that answers will "always" be found elsewhere because those created by Africans are viewed as... inferior, if not irrelevant?

Anyone who has created a prototype or a notion that purports to defy the laws of physics, mathematics, etc., is always open to criticism. Such a person is frequently seen as mad and unworthy of attention. People criticising science overlook its complexity since it is static and dynamic. In other words, science is always full of surprises, most of which eventually make sense. Do you recall the geocentric theory, which claimed that the earth was the universe's centre of gravity? How many people were expelled or threatened with death at that time because they understood the Ptolemaic or geocentric model of the universe was an anomaly thanks to scientific observation and models? At the time, doing so was considered a scientific and theological heresy! Contradictory to scientific truth and religion at the time was harmful. However, with our telescopes and satellites, it is now clear to practically everyone that this hypothesis was illogical. As one can see, this absurdity was taken as "truth" for ages. The above examples remind us to maintain our humility regarding scientific findings. Indeed, what may appear absurd by today's science standards may be so tomorrow, and another will eventually supersede this reality. But why do Africans feel inferior, and why is Africa developing slowly?

One of the reasons for this inferiority complex, though not the only one, is the mental legacy of colonialism. Since, strangely, patriotism is not appreciated when it comes to encouraging creativity in fields related to science and technology in Africa, changing this mentality is a complex undertaking. Now, discussing Africa's rise and industrialisation is one thing, bestowing honours here and there and posing for photos beside winners and runners-up at mediatised events. The critical query, however, is how many of those who have received political praise will receive financial support to enable mass production of their breakthroughs or inventions and to make Africans proud to use and buy things developed in Africa by Africans. The answer to the previous query appears to be: essentially none. If not, Africa would have already experimented with producing energy from plants, air or oxygen from trees. But perhaps thinking that way is crazy after all.

In the minds of other Africans, aren't African scientists too intellectually constrained to create complex systems that can generate electricity? How many Africans have already created agricultural machinery that could aid in mechanising African agriculture? They are countless, even though many African nations have made agriculture a strategic economic sector or priority. Africans who possess the knowledge and abilities to mechanise agriculture with little assistance from foreign sources, hence at a lower cost, are not the ones that rulers pay attention to help them to materialise their constructive ideas. As a result, agriculture is not mechanised, and the agro-processing sector, an extension of agriculture, has not been fully developed. Even the most intelligent Africans have a persistent misconception that science and technology can only advance in the industrialised world. Therefore, even considering that an African would make a needle using an African's industrial machinery is absurd! Geographically, commercially, and economically, Africans are viewed as little more than consumers of goods made elsewhere. They must continue to be consumers and under no circumstances producers of the goods they are now importing! Therefore, when African leaders claim that their content has to industrialise, what kind of industrialisation are they referring to? They are accountable for conveying the correct message about the real purpose of automation. An African genius might be valued in a variety of ways.

Let's look at the instance of Arthur Zang from Cameroon, the creator of an ECG (electrocardiogram) tablet. Why aren't more hospitals in Cameroon and Africa using this effective tool that has the potential to save many lives? Not to add that the device's price is more than reasonable and might be lowered in the future. Industrialisation would include, among other things, aiding the inventor financially and diplomatically to ensure that Cameroon develops the capacity to produce the majority of the parts required to assemble the gadgets locally rather than having them made abroad. The educational system would also have begun collaborating with Arthur Zang, so Cameroonian students could become familiar with the courses the inventor had to take from India (remote learning) to create his initial prototype. The illustration above is the most excellent method for a productive workforce that needs training to address local issues. Industrialisation would also mean that Cameroon would have started a diplomatic effort in Africa to promote a device that is one of the best inventions in the healthcare sector globally and then assist the inventor in signing contracts in other African nations.

Indeed, it is well-known that certain Western Europeans have a racist ideology that views Africans as inferior beings. Undeniably, most Africans have consciously or unconsciously accepted the stigma of inferiority. The claim that Western European colonisation and the Christianization of Africans harmed their psyches is unavoidably true. The African seemed to have lost confidence and despised her traditional traditions, which has led to devaluing those valued and genuinely indigenous virtues that could help her situation. Among other evils, this issue results from the interconnected pressures of colonisation, Christianization, Islamization, and, most importantly, the slave trade. The saying that Africa is in a pickle is well-known. Africans and non-Africans concur that Africa is underdeveloped, retrograde, and lagging behind other nations in every aspect of society. While reading or watching mass media, especially media of foreign origin, it is easy to think that Africa is a pit of moral decay where raping, women beating, human trafficking, especially child trafficking, baby factories, ritual killings, etc., are the norm. It is claimed that religious intolerance and fanaticism affect perceptions and behaviour in Africa, where authorities prefer to kill innocent people rather than cede control when the time is right. Teenagers are reportedly exploited as child soldiers. It is an ill, impoverished continent that is even more helpless than it already is. It is a continent that is portrayed as being dark, and it is, in fact, black. The question, therefore, becomes: Is Africa as gloomy and hopeless as it is supposed to be? What led to such a representation, once more and fundamentally? This essay claims that Africa is not entirely as shown above and may have a brighter future. Additionally, external reasons rather than internal ones led to the impulse to define Africa as in the preceding. By "external factors," we refer to Europeans' involvement in slavery and the slave trade in Africa, the continent's division, colonialism, imperialism and its offshoot, capitalism, which have completely exploited the continent. On the other hand, internal factors pertain to the claim that Africans are mostly to blame for the continent's problems. It is crucial to see Africa in her heyday before things start falling apart for her due to external reasons before attempting to identify the origins of her dilemma. One might easily forget or not know that Africa formerly had a significant role in the origins and progression of humanity, as well as in the actualisation of humanity's civilisation, based on the impression of Africa presented in the introduction notes above. Because of her enormous and everlasting contributions to human civilisation, Oguejiofor makes the following claim: "There is no longer any debate among scientists as to the fact that Africa is the origin of the human race and that homo sapiens first appeared there many hundreds of thousands of years ago, well before the Neanderthal epoch in Europe. Africa also served as the starting point for human, and technical development, beginning with the development of wooden and bone implements and ending with the historic transition into the stone era. Oguejiorfor (2001) "It is important to note, argues Obafemi Awolowo, "that the use of stone tools was a technical revolution among the primitive people of the old, middle and new stone age, and that, in this revolution, Africa was clearly in the lead." Neopaleolithic Africa eventually transitioned into the agricultural and pastoral periods, followed by the iron age. It created steel by 600 BC, referred to as "possibly the best steel in the world at the time, and unquestionably equal to or even better than the steel produced in early modern Europe" (24). Oguejiofor continues his apologies by asserting that ancient civilisations like Egypt, Kush, Napata and Meroe, Nubia, and Axum flourished on the African continent. The African continent was travelling toward civilisation at the same time as the rest of the world during the height of the civilisations mentioned earlier. The thriving Christianity that gave rise to figures like Augustine, Origen, Athanasius, Clement of Alexandria, and many others began in northern Africa. In the same way that the expansionist Islam undermined the successes of Christianity in its northern territory, the area also served as a solid foundation for the growth of Islam and its subsequent extension south of the Sahara. The continent could boast nations and empires such as Ghana, Mali, Songhai, Akan, Mossi, Oyo, Benin, Hausa, Congo, Ouadai, Darfur, Funji, Ethiopia, Zimbabwe and so on from the 7th century AD to the present. Many of these governments and empires initially experienced the virile stages of evolution, then achieved their apogees and fell into collapse long before the continent experienced the worst atrocities in its history. Others crossed the threshold of modernity only to be swept away by the flood of history, which they were powerless to withstand and whose force was amplified by both the unique circumstances of their existence and their unintentional involvement in it (Oguejiofor 24–25). What then overshadowed that brilliance after this depiction of African history? How is it that today, especially in the West, Africa is connected with everything negative to the point where Africans adopt such a pessimistic outlook? How are they accepting such a pessimistic outlook?

Our role models, such as our teachers, mentors and leaders, unknowingly instructed other young people to feel inferior and maintain that inferiority. We were indoctrinated to feel inadequate and have low self-esteem, just like many young people in Nigeria today. Here are a few instances. Thoughtless instruction was given to us (and is still given to children today) that "oyibobundimuo," "oyibobuagbara," and "America iluoba" (which implies that white men's nation is the land of kings naturally) and "oyibobundimuo" "white men are natural spirits," and "white men are wizards by nature." We were brainlessly taught that practically everything "black" is necessarily evil, as youngsters are still being brainlessly taught today. In fact, according to our "educators," it is OK to refer to evil as being "black" (the moniker given to persons of African descent). According to this doctrine, a lousy individual is the "black sheep of the family" They ought to be "blacklisted." According to this school of thought, the unlawful market is the "black market" (as though only black people conduct business there). According to this doctrine, Satan is "black" in colour, although no one has ever seen him. According to our "learned" teachers, the frequent usage of the colour "black" to represent evil demonstrates a command of "Queen's

English". It is deserving of an "A" in the English essay composition. A wonderful education! It's too bad!

Moreover, it is crucial to note that the governmental fragmentation that was a drawback of ancient Africa's history is what initially allowed European encroachment on the continent. In contrast, most African political groups had modest, perhaps tiny territorial scopes. The distinctive aspect of the African phenomena of slavery is not only that it existed but rather the fact that it was only in Africa that enormous swaths of an entire continent's people were, up until far into the nineteenth century, scattered in their millions as slaves to far-off regions of the world. The "most iniquitous transaction in human history" has thus been appropriately described as the African slave trade. This specific occurrence came with baggage that Africans suffered through. The slave trade cultivated an atmosphere of violence and unrest in Africa. It worked against the factors that may have ensured the continent's stability, especially as the victims of this heinous trade were young people in the prime of their life. The millions of individuals transported away in their numbers represented a horrible destruction of the productive capacity. Wars that had as their goal the capture of enslaved people or other contraband caused enormous upheaval in social and economic life. As a result, no environment was favourable for a peaceful existence, let alone growth. The slave trade left fear, social unrest, bloodshed and political instability behind.

In conclusion, "Slave trading pushed Africa farther into the valley of underdevelopment and contributed to the West's industrialisation. According to legend, the West Coast of Africa resembled Europe in certain ways when the first Europeans arrived there, but today, the situation is the opposite. Africa lags behind the US, Europe and even a few of the then-classified as impoverished nations. The phenomena of the division of Africa followed fast on the heels of the slave trade in Africa. Partition was "arranged and given 'legitimacy' by the Berlin conference in 1885. It meant a further round of destruction, neglect and degradation of things African—art and craft, language and oral literature as well as social, political and religious institutions" (32 Oguejiofor). As a result, it had the crippling consequence that "With the partition of Africa, different ethnic groups and nations suddenly became parts of the same political entities without any regard to their history, religion, culture or experience". The act was carried out here. The division of Africa has led to concerns about ethnic and religious prejudice. Africans nowadays are so aware of their ethnic and religious differences that every problem is seen in terms of those divisions. A typical African finds it challenging to communicate their thoughts or sentiments without some tinge of ethnic or religious allegiance.

Regarding factors contributing to Africa's negative outlook among other nations brought on by the European invasion, religious chauvinism outweighs ethnicism. The sense that religions have come to characterise Africa is numerous and controversial within a specific ethnic group. Because of the ontological significance, all-pervading, and being-to-being binding nature of religion in general, which led Achebe to compare the devastating nature of European penetration into Africa to faith, it has won our brothers, and our clan can no longer function as a cohesive group.

On the contrary, how can the African claim to be on par with the daunting scientific and technological advancements of the West, and when will he match such achievements, one would wonder. The African must comfort himself with the knowledge that, historically, his ancestors were the envy of the West due to their countless accomplishments; as a result, Africa is known as the cradle of civilisation. He shouldn't constantly be mourning the prevalence of the slave trade and conquering. The fact that all previous world empires have fallen, and Africa is no exception, should help her start developing self-confidence. She should be pleased that the so-called developed countries sourced their raw resources from Africa. Extension of it, African leaders should be motivated to put measures in place to create favourable conditions to eschew being servants to the Western powers. Then, they can compete with and perhaps surpass their Western counterparts in science and technology.Evidentially, the accomplishments of countless Africans, such as Philip Emeagwali, who are dispersed throughout Europe, motivate us that Africa can do well when we consciously set our priorities right. After gaining confidence, the African must take action by going within to uncover the qualities that set him apart from others and can provide him with the means for growth and eventual recognition and admiration by the rest of the world. These are indigenous African ideals. Do Africans hold such values, and if so, what values? In addition to the racist stereotypes that Africans lack reason, it is important to emphasise the fallacy of such presumptions by pointing out that Ramose's research shows that Africans share this human trait universally. Kofi Annan's success in peaceful rural diplomacy in his native Ghana has been largely credited by many detractors for one of his diplomatic triumphs: reaching an agreement with Iraq on the United Nations weapons inspection regime. This illustration means that occasionally, village diplomacy can prevent avoidable war between nations. The example mentioned above disproves the claim that Africans lack reason. It also highlights the importance of the African village's quiet diplomacy, demonstrating that problems are not always settled through force or bloodshed. It is a value of extended conversations among Africans, which are sometimes described as tedious but ultimately provide the desired outcome. This value must be revived to resolve the many conflicts ravaging the African continent, which appears to be eroding in favour of quick manipulations and manoeuvres imported from the West. Western manipulation and manoeuvring seem to only provide temporary relief from the conflicts rather than providing them with lasting resolutions. The fact that Africans have an inferiority complex is the worst aspect of their situation due to the European invasion. And this complication is a mental health concern. Africans' ideas were shaped by Europeans, who helped keep them in their current position. The African needs to refocus his thoughts to counter the tide. Africans must therefore embrace more radical and critical reasoning in their approach to life's difficulties. In addition to those mentioned above, traditional African ideals, most African countries' educational systems must be reorganised in response to this attitude change. To help African children develop the habit of critical thinking early on, curriculum designers should incorporate aspects of philosophy that have been simplified for understanding at the primary school level. Since philosophy has the unique power to ignite critical thinking in people, the policy should be altered to allow philosophy departments to open at African colleges where there are none currently. Again, teaching the history of Africa as a continent and the history of the various African nations would help Africans understand who they are and what must be done. African awareness should permeate formal and informal education across the continent to foster a more radical and critical mindset among Africans. This mentality has the unfortunate side effect of making Africans no longer see things through the prism of their specific ethnic or religious interests in their respective countries but rather through the periscope of national interests following a thorough discussion free from inequality, restriction of freedom and hostile manipulations. Similar to how they'll see situations on the continent from pan-African perspectives rather than just those of their nations of origin. The advantage of this mindset is that it would promote long-needed unity among Africans. Africans can thus address problems objectively without leaning toward those dividing ideologies imposed by the West, thanks to their togetherness. Therefore, this mindset will do away with the ethnic and religious divisions ingrained in Africans' minds and prevent them from thinking past those boundaries, keeping them eternally down. Africans can start to free themselves from the extra apron if they adopt this mentality. With this perspective, Africans can start to free themselves from the useless ties that the Europeans have around their necks, which have forced them into a dreadful corner and caused them to be described in the most horrifying ways. In this approach, the plight of Africa might be improved and transformed into an advantage for the continent.

Consider the question: Where are the "Greeks of old"? How did the ancient Romans fare? Where are the Turks of the Ottoman Empire? Who can recall the Greek, Roman, or Ottoman empires today, although they were great empire builders and international leaders? But does this put the British and Americans, whose empires are still strong or relatively modern, ahead of their descendants? Global Africa, please hasten. Nobody is better than us. We are God's special creation with unique skills, preferences, and manners. Therefore, we don't need to bleach our skin and look like Europeans in order to feel human.

We don't have to have long nail extensions like witches and eagles to feel posh. We don't have to flee into Whiteness to escape ourselves. We already qualify as beings of humanity. So, be authentic. You're from Africa. You are special. Be at ease with your skin. Be proud of where nature placed you as an African; enjoy your life and let others live theirs. That is how nature operates. We must embrace a particular lifestyle to maintain excellence in every aspect of our lives as producers. If we invested in cutting-edge technological education, international best practices for professionalism and creative thinking, we as a continent would become economically active and a significant player in international economics. A technology-driven economy where speed is the game's name, a strategic marketing mindset and contemporary innovations would result in a much more dynamic and productive economy. These factors include high-quality goods, services, standards, professionalism and a superior mentality that is competitive enough to sell our products globally. However, Africa has to create institutions where professionalism is a way of life and pass laws that ensure that inferiority and mediocrity are not tolerated. To become the world's envy, we must embrace a motto: "If it's fake, it's not Africa." Genuine quality may be sold to anyone, regardless of colour, race, or tribe. Results, after all, don't lie! In conclusion, Africans can take their future seriously if they choose to because all of the natural resources on this continent should be taken and processed there as evidence of her industrialisation. Industrialisation is one of the fastest ways for Africa to thrive. The scientific and technological innovations required to industrialise Africa can be created there, where researchers and scientists with few resources are still developing creative solutions that African governments can afford. They must not hold the view that Africans are simply talented athletes, singers, poets, comedians and dancers. They are top-notch researchers with theories that can challenge our preconceptions about science and technology. For this reason, "mental liberation" is the first step in developing the industrialisation process.

CHAPTER 4
ASSUMPTION PHENOMENON

In our quest to discover truth, knowledge, and wisdom, the mind sometimes plays the game of probability. Thus, to what extent does something qualifies to be truth, to what percentage does something fit fixed criteria to exist in its form, and what are the chances that something is really what it is but not something else? Thus, the game of thinking critically about things, guessing and constructing hypothetical views toward issues, problems and solutions is essential as one aims to pursue knowledge and solve problems. Necessity is the mother of invention, but it takes presupposition about how something can become something else to materialise into a good idea that fits necessity to yield creation.

An assumption is a belief that requires in-depth analysis; it's what we believe consciously or unconsciously without evidence. Our judgements, often called inferences, frequently rest on unquestioning presumptions. Our cultures, ideas, and values as people hook us onto a core set of presumptions either consciously or unconsciously (Paradigmatic assumptions); for example, a person from America may consider kissing in public as a way of expressing love, whiles some countries may consider it as indecorous, one may also see a career job as a ticket you subscribe to keep you in the category of a middle-class income earner. Others may also perceive a career job as a platform that prepares one to be time-conscious, harness capabilities and improve one working skills: which will be advantageous toward one ambition to start a productive project or venture into entrepreneurship. In addition, customs, values, schools of thought and cultures develop one mentally and socially, leading to differences in how one critically analyses situations and issues. One starts questioning the relevance of some creatures, ideologies, systems and inventions. Extension of it, one accepts what one perceives as crucial based on one's reasoning. This illustration is known as prescriptive assumption explaining how one suggests what he thinks about how things should be done. For example, one may indicate that primary and high school authorities should reduce subject courses for students not geared towards what they aspire to be or the career they dream of pursuing. Others may also suggest that most subjects for primary and High school students prepare them to be mentally tough and expose them to at least an excerpt of knowledge in other fields.

The prescriptive assumption tends to partially or fully answer how opinionated one may be toward a situation. More or less, the primary method in psychology to study opinions through observation results in prescriptive assumption as one tries to find explanations to arrive at an idea. The causal assumption is also a type of assumption that focuses on how things work and how one can impact those processes. Notably, all these assumptions are interconnected as one expresses views, feelings, opinions and suggestions in day-to-day activities. Assumptions are essential as it leads a learner, researcher or scientist to land on their target goal through careful processes and techniques. Everyone is free to think and, conversely, free to assume. However, the distinction and standards that differentiate assumption from truth and fact should be highly considered. Most importantly, one can only be sure of the authenticity of one's assumption after undertaking research that unveils elucidated evidence about the subject under an analysis of which one presumed.

But a critical thinker is aware of these assumptions since they may be false or inaccurate. Just because we assume something to be true doesn't mean it is. Be aware of your assumptions and those of others when acquiring and analysing information. We frequently assume that what we perceive is the reality. What makes this a problem? You probably don't agree with some people or beliefs in your community, at work, or home. Conflict will inevitably arise as your perspective and another person intersect or interject. This hypothesis is observable in news reports, politics, religion, and sports organisations. Most of these disagreements start without any formal meetings or verbal communication. They take place in the mind and are driven by presumptions. That refers to presumptions about the motivations and processes behind another person's ideas and behaviour. We make up reasons as to why we disagree with someone's viewpoint.

The narrative built on assumptions is what most sharply divides us. They allow us to treat individuals like ordinary objects. If you disagree with me, you are either insane, lying, or stupid (disconnected from reality). Ironically, my self-imposed ignorance, dishonesty, and even psychosis are at their height because of my presumptive idea that I am the root of all problems and misunderstandings. Probably the only thing keeping it from being labelled as harmful is how widespread it is. Why do we assume things? When are they useful, and why do they cause issues? For instance, I was swiftly passed in the right lane while driving last week. Faster drivers are expected to pass on the left in the US (for you British-born drivers). Wasn't the other car's driver careless, haughty, and disobeying the law? I once had a manager who would point out even the smallest errors in the documents and briefs I would prepare. He didn't like me. In her eyes, nothing I did was acceptable!

I frequently disagree with my coworker on how to prepare for the events we attend. He is discussing nothing. In these situations, I thought—indeed, I was convinced—that the way I saw the situation (or the person) was the only possible scenario. Have you ever dealt with cases like this? What information did you possess about the situation at the time? What do you think the truth was? There could have been a different perspective. We frequently develop assumptions because they help us process the outside world. The huge neural network in the brain requires enormous amounts of energy to function, claims a Yale neurobiology professor: About 100 billion cells make up our brains, and each one connects to other brain cells more than 10,000 times. The enormous variety of possible cell connection configurations makes higher-order thinking possible, but this presents a huge energy cost problem for evolution. The brain must effectively encode information in order to conserve energy. The act of making assumptions is one way our brain saves energy. To identify patterns in how the world functions, we lean on our prior experiences. When we encounter new circumstances, we adapt these patterns—or presumptions— to the unique setting. This method spares us the effort of re-examining every case from scratch. And it's frequently quite helpful! For instance, I can presume that my attire to work last week will also be appropriate this week. Then choosing what to wear to work doesn't need much thought. Now, when are assumptions problematic? As Jack Colwell and Chip Huth point out, "Assumptions start causing problems when we believe our way of interpreting a given situation is the only way to analyse that situation" (Jack Colwell and Chip Huth 2019). Hence, anyone who does not see things our way is somehow "less than others"; They are ignorant, foolish, or simply wrong. Every person brings their own experiences and background regarding human relations to shape how they see things. Assuming that our way of seeing is the sole way to see is almost always incorrect.

Furthermore, we encourage conflict when we categorise others who disagree with us and add judgment to our assumptions. Imagine becoming the target of an assumption-based judgemental comment. The second person can say, "I'm confident X happened," when two people are talking about an incident that occurred. You're mistaken! Which kind of reaction do you think you'll most likely make? What sort of connection is the other person proposing to you? However, how often do we catch they are ignorant, foolish, or wrong? Every person brings their own experiences and background regarding human relations to shape how they see things. Assuming that our way of seeing is the sole way to see is almost always incorrect.

Furthermore, we encourage conflict when we categorise others who disagree with us and add judgment to our assumptions. Imagine becoming the target of an assumption-based judgemental comment. The second person can say, "I'm confident X happened," when two people are talking about an incident that occurred. You're mistaken! Which kind of reaction do you think you'll most likely make? What sort of connection is the other person proposing to you? However, how often do we catch it? To help ourselves avoid making problematic assumptions, we can get profoundly and genuinely curious about the situation or person we're encountering. We can ask ourselves what might be going on for the other person. How might they see things? What else could be true? Simply asking questions like these helps us stay open to the possibility that our truth isn't the only truth. With this openness, we automatically believe: The way I see something is one way of perceiving it; how I feel about someone is how I think; The way I remember an event is my memory of that event and not its entirety.

Owing to this, how best can the people in Africa learn the nitty gritty of assumptions so it does not become a problem or a phenomenon? Assumptions can also be points in an argument that a writer takes for granted and does not prove with evidence. Sometimes, due to selfish reasons or how unprofessional one may be, one can merge assumptions with bias. Bias can be based on assumptions, as a person's preconceived notions or beliefs may lead them to make biased decisions or interpretations. In Africa, problems like bribery, Corruption, and nepotism are common due to unenforced laws on the government side and a lack of patriotism and discipline at large. Also, from a psychological point of view, causal assumption and assumption bias psych citizens to keep on involved in corrupt activities. For example, a government official may take a bribe and assume that other generals on top are richer because they take a bribe.

A manager will consider employing an unqualified person who is related to him and would not see anything wrong because he assumes that's the norm everywhere. Even though one may be right towards one assumption in such a scenario, the right motivation is that change starts from one person before taking over an entire country. Bias assumptions in such systems will only motivate one to be more corrupt as it backs up one selfish interest instead of the country's future. Normalising such acts is a canker that must be frowned upon in Africa. It will be relevant when the youth in Africa renew their mindset and have Africa at heart, and eschew malpractices that will threaten the growth and development of Africa. Factually, rich cultures in different parts of the world that one sees its shining stars had scars in their history. For that matter, the current underdeveloped state of Africa should not discourage Africans from holding on firmly to the flag of patriotism, hope and determination towards a suitable course to effect change in Africa.

If there must be any development in Africa, it will require getting good checks and balances, which could guard how we see things as accurate and the need to realise if it's true with satisfactory proof.

Evidence illustrates that when horrible acts occur in Africa, people tend to think there is no such place with imperfections rather than looking for ways to prevent or stop them. The above is one of the problematic issues of assumption. Because there are corrupt individuals globally, we shouldn't encourage individuals in Africa to remain corrupt because this could hinder Africa's development. Corruption continues to harm Africa, hampering democracy, growth and the ability to bring people out of poverty. The continent ranks lowest amongst global regions in the Corruption Perceptions Index (CPI), our ranking of 180 countries by their perceived levels of public sector corruption. African countries average 32 out of 100 in their CPI scores, and six out of the bottom ten are African. Sin has an influence that cannot be understated. While over $50 billion in stolen goods leave Africa annually, around 43% of Africans live in poverty. Funding might go toward social services and employment opportunities, which are the areas where more funding is most required. From Zimbabwe to Libya, the lack of growth is exacerbated by pervasive corruption schemes that scare away investors and stifle future development. In Africa, misappropriated monies are responsible for a 25% reduction in development funding. Families and individuals are also impacted negatively. One out of two individuals in Sub-Saharan Africa admitted to paying bribes for land services, such as registering property and preventing the confiscation of their family houses. According to research, more than half of all citizens believe that Corruption is getting worse in their nation and that their government is doing a poor job of combating it; according to the research, bribing increases yearly among individuals who use public services, including health care and education. This analysis translates to roughly 130 million people living in the 35 nations studied. The Global Corruption Barometer (GCB), carried out in collaboration with Afrobarometer and Omega Research in 2019, is the most extensive and thorough study of African residents' perceptions of Corruption and their personal experiences with bribes. The study includes the opinions of almost 47,000 people from 35 different African nations. Citizens think the police are the most corrupt institution, with 47% believing that most police are corrupt. These results are consistent with findings from the 2015 report. Unsurprisingly, police also consistently earn the highest bribery rate across Africa. Other public services like utilities, electricity and water, identification documents, licenses and passports also have high bribery rates. The problem in Africa is the corruption chain. Citizens think their leaders are corrupt and unwilling to change the course of action. They also tend to follow suit, considering that the moment you dare to be different, you will not enjoy the national coffers too, and will eventually swim in poverty. The query is, is this assumption wrong if national development must supersede individuals' interests?

When you ask the majority of people why underdeveloped countries are poor, what comes to mind? We're relatively sure that Corruption will be involved. Corruption consistently ranks as the most popular reason why poverty persists, whether you ask hundreds of individuals in a nationally representative survey or a few people in intimate focus groups. Ten years of research on how people view poverty has found that Corruption is the only issue related to it that the general public is eager to discuss. However, it is also strange because those genuinely involved in development want to talk about it the least and don't bring up corruption issues for discussion; it feels like we are trapped in some grandiose Basil Faulty parody. If development organisations are serious about winning the public debate on aid, which many do not, then we must face the spectre of Corruption. Integrity Action, Global Integrity, the Tax Justice Network, Transparency International, and ONE, to mention a few, are doing excellent work in openness and accountability. But Corruption is always an unaddressed issue; there is an understandable reluctance among those involved in development to educate the public about the complexities of Corruption in developing nations. The popular image of Corruption is an African dictator's family plundering public coffers to purchase Michael Jackson memorabilia, fast cars, fine wines, and mansions. The reality of everyday life is much more complicated and routine. Poor people frequently turn to Corruption as a (flawed) solution to various issues, including security issues and access to essential services. And it often entails the cooperation of wealthy nations and fraudulent billing by international corporations. The most vulnerable people lose. Africans should understand that irrespective of the fact that specific individuals are amassing wealth at the detriment of the nation and continent at large should not deter us from daring to be different to change the course of time if the unborn generations benefit from our continental development. As a famous funny quote goes, "In Japan, a corrupt person kills himself; in China, they kill him; in Europe, they jail him; but in Africa, he presents himself for election". The above concept should not be the ideal situation in Africa. There should be a wake-up call to chastise our behaviour and toughen our mentality to think critically about how ubiquitous these uncouth assumptions are and the need to relinquish or cut their source and acts.

At independence, most African countries were presented with an opportunity to chart new directions in their development agenda to improve the livelihoods of their people. The policy agenda of all African states at independence was mainly to fight ignorance, poverty and diseases. However, to date, all African countries are still experiencing low levels of development characterised by high levels of poverty, unemployment, insecurity and general social and moral decay. All these developmental problems are partly blamed on bad governance and, more particularly, misrule and high levels of Corruption the continent is experiencing. Indeed, the case of Africa is a paradox in that although it is the richest in the world in terms of natural resources, it remains at the bottom of the global governance and development prism. Professor Patrice Lumumba once said, "Corruption is something we talk about, it's something we complain about, it is something whose negative impact we recognise, it is something that even the corrupt acknowledges it's a bad thing but the irony and the tragedy at once, is that those who engage in Corruption loves it. The tragedy at once is that those of us who do not engage in it directly accommodate it". Our level of tolerance for Corruption in Africa is sky-high! A Long time ago, a great Greek philosopher said, "It is a disease in nature of man to hang the small thieves and to elect the great ones into public office". We do that in Kenya, Uganda, Tanzania and Africa, so Africa remains the poorest continent. Looking at Africa, the wealthiest men and women occupy public offices. We live in a continent where we celebrate thieves and vilify good men and women; that is the tragedy of Africa.

When every other continent in the recent past has moved in the right direction, Africa remains, in the words of Tony B., "the scar in the conscience of humanity". Corruption is worse than prostitution. The latter might endanger an individual's morals, but the former invariably endangers the morals of an entire country. The trouble with Corruption is not its presence. After all, every country in the world has to deal with the scourge of Corruption at some level. The problem with Corruption in Africa is that it has become so pervasive and pernicious that it has become a way of life. In all African countries, one can say that the corrupt are canonised, and anti-corruption warriors are demonised.

Corruption has become so omnipresent in Africa. It has left nothing untouched in its wake. The corrupt, the children of darkness, are found in every sector of our society. They are in the Executive arm of the government, the Legislature, the Judiciary, among health workers, in agriculture, in Churches, in the Mosques, in the Temples - everywhere. Indeed, one can dare say that those who choose to stand in the way of the train of Corruption are courting suicide; the person is like an oasis in the desert, an island in the vast ocean. Therefore, the person's chances of survival in Africa are like a snowball in hell. The irony and the paradox at once is that the most outstanding practitioners of Corruption admit that it is a vice that must be fought. The tragedy, however, is that they say with their mouths what they do not believe in their hearts. Let them say what they want; history has repeatedly shown that Corruption is cancer that consumes society and those who engage in it. Our task today is straightforward but holy. We are here to remind the presidents, ministers, mayors, district commissioners, agricultural officers, health care providers, cleaners, and everyone else that the creed of greed will destroy us all and that we must now take a moment to pause and consider King Solomon's timeless wisdom from Ecclesiastes 3:1-8, which states that there is a time for everything. There is a time for everything and a season for every activity under heaven:

- A time to be born and a time to die.

- A time to plant and a time to uproot.

- A time to kill and a time to heal.

- A time to tear down and a time to build.

- A time to weep and a time to laugh.

- A time to mourn and a time to dance.

- A time to scatter stones and a time to gather them.

- A time to embrace and a time to refrain.

- A time to search and a time to give up.

- A time to keep and a time to throw away.

- A time to tear and a time to mend.

- A time to be silent and a time to speak.

- A time to love and hate and for war and peace.

" The root causes of Corruption vary from place to place depending on the political, social, economic and cultural circumstances. In Africa, some of the identifiable causes of Corruption include the negative colonial legacy, poor leadership, politics of the belly, omnipotent state, greed and selfishness, clientelism and patronage nepotism, absence of popular participation of the public in government, weak institutions of governance, lack of accountability and transparency, lack of political will, soft ethical values, centralist nature of the state and concentration of state power, weak judicial system and constant insecurity and conflicts. The words of Chinua Achebe are unambiguous on the effects of Corruption in Africa; he said: Without doubt, Corruption has permeated the African society, and anyone who can say that Corruption in Africa has not become alarming is either a fool, a crook or else does not live in this continent. Evidence in developing countries indicates that Corruption negatively affects growth and development. In the words of Kofi Annan, the former United Nations Secretary-General: "Corruption undermines economic performance, weakens democratic institutions and the rule of law, disrupts social order and destroys public trust, thus allowing organised crime, terrorism and other threats to human security to flourish…And it is always the public good that suffers." (Kofi Anan, 2004, UNCAC) The words of Hugh Bayley succinctly capture the effects of Corruption in Africa; he says: "Corruption is bleeding Africa to death, and the cost is borne by the poor. Some estimates put money corruptly, leaving the continent at greater risk. Much of the money is banked in Britain or our overseas territories and dependencies, and sometimes British citizens or companies are involved in corrupt deals. The African continent needs its governments in power to get tough on corruption". Hugh Bayley, (2006)

From a logical standpoint, combating Corruption requires multidisciplinary, interdisciplinary strategies concentrating on its political, economic, legal, administrative, social, and moral aspects. Using comprehensive, consistent, broad-based approaches with a long-term outlook is vital. According to some, eliminating poor governance is a more fundamental aspect of fighting Corruption than catching corrupt people. Examining how political parties are funded and carefully regulated is a crucial first step in combating Corruption in the countries of Africa. Undeniably, single parties ruled the majority of African nations for a considerable amount of time after gaining independence. The ANC, which has been in power in South Africa since the regime of apartheid was overthrown in 1994, is the most recent typical example. Kenya African National Union (KANU) was the country's ruling party from its independence in 1963 until 2002. Since Tanzania's independence, it has been led by Chama Cha Mapinduzi

(CCM). Political leaders must set an example by practising "servant leadership," refraining from using rhetoric, double speak, and communicating in codes when combating political Corruption. Instead, they should establish and practice strong policies addressing corruption and party and state governance and encourage excellent values and morals in the political system and the larger population. In order to pursue contracts with the government, the business sector, which represents the supply side of Corruption, must also abide by the established "integrity" requirements. Once again, it must be acknowledged that Corruption has a disproportionately negative impact on the poor's quality of life because it jeopardises the provision of public services (such as housing, water, and health care), diverts funds and other resources (that could have been used for development, job creation, and poverty alleviation), weakens the ability of the state to provide effective services equally, and erodes the democratic system's legitimacy (citizens' trust in the government). To clearly demonstrate that the general public, particularly the underprivileged, voiceless, and defenceless, are the main victims of Corruption, this myth must be disproved. In addition to being a crime against humanity, Corruption also violates human rights. Corruption in Zimbabwe, Kenya, and Nigeria is to blame for the myriad conflicts in many African regions. The recent "revolutions" in Egypt and Tunisia have also been investigated for Corruption and bad governance. Declaring Corruption, a national calamity that has damaged and will continue to undermine our development efforts to reduce poverty and misery among our people, is one crucial tactic for inspiring a concerted national reaction to the vice. All African governments must lead in organising local, regional, and global responses to Corruption through efficient management, prevention, awareness-raising, and enforcement. This project might assist in putting an end to the risky defensiveness and, in some cases, denialist attitudes that exist in some political and administrative circles regarding the extent of Corruption.

In order to promote the greater good of society, political parties must be appropriately organised and managed. Political parties must abide by the established laws, rules, and conventions of society or a nation in order to pursue such a route. Nations that do not yet have laws and systems governing political parties must do so immediately in order to promote public interest, ensure fair and effective representation, control party funding, restructure party management, and ensure transparency and accountability in party and national affairs. The parties themselves must penalise the poor behaviour of their leaders and members and promote good behaviour on a legal, social, and political level. If it's done in front of the public, the government will regain its moral standing and be able to deal with crimes respectably committed by the common people.

Additionally, it will assist in enforcing the rules among common people. The parties must continuously install new leadership at all more capable and sincere levels. The internal party elections must be conducted on a merit-based basis. Competence, moral character, and dedication to public service must all be considered when evaluating candidates.

In a nutshell, during the past 50 years, Africa has gained a reputation for being rife with Corruption and impunity. Africans continue to be the least understood people and the least known continent. This story is being told because she (Africa) won't share her experience. As Chinua Achebe famously put it, "The exploits of the hunter rather than the bravery of the lion will always be talked about as long as lions do not have their historians." Today, Africa is glaringly absent from the international media, controlled by American,

European, and increasingly Chinese channels. The much-touted Agenda 2063, which aims to launch African nations into the orbit of development, won't succeed unless Africans actively promote and support it. Africans should promote using facts and reality to advance the continent rather than making assumptions, consciously or unconsciously. Africa must experience peace, swiftness, deterrence, and conflict or phenomenon resolution.

REASONING AND CRITICAL THINKING

One of the body's most powerful organs is the human brain. The brain, a three-pound organ that houses intelligence, acts as an interpreter of the senses, a behavioural controller, and a movement-initiating mechanism in humans, enabling them to live successfully in their settings. The pinnacle of biological evolution is the brain, which makes intellect, memory, movement, and emotions possible through complex processes. Since the brain comprises roughly 100 billion microscopic cells called neurons, it is a tremendously potent tool for survival.

The brain's function includes:

- Speech and language processing.

- Automatic behaviour.

- Memories and emotions.

- Human thoughts and decisions.

Contrarily, conscience, understanding, and reasoning are all part of the mind. One's capacity to think, feel, and participate in physical activities.

From a biological perspective, the limbic system is responsible for human survival regarding our behavioural and emotional responses, nutrition, reproduction, and fight-or-flight reactions. The brain's cerebral cortex is responsible for many cognitive and sensory processes, including learning, problem-solving, emotions, consciousness, and memory. When solving problems, reasoning plays a significant role in the process. Making decisions, forecasting results, or developing explanations based on already available knowledge are all reasoning examples. Also, thinking involves making decisions based on information rather than acting quickly or impulsively.

From a psychological standpoint, one needs a reason to rule one's surroundings and address environmental issues. Everyone makes decisions regularly, whether they are necessary or not. Even when one approaches a decision critically, some occasionally do not seem evident. For instance, choosing what to dress, what shoes to wear, and what hairstyle to wear for a particular occasion. Reasoning and critical thinking are utilised when making decisions about everyday matters like those mentioned above, such as what to wear in light of the weather. It takes evidence to persuade people of your intuitions and beliefs, even in casual conversations. Even though speaking is difficult, thinking is required to express one word. To effectively communicate with an audience and enable a listener to infer the exceptions to poetic literacy in a message, one's reasoning skills are helpful, especially when the speaker is "Shakespeare." Living things' primary objective is to survive successfully in their surroundings. As a result, when making decisions, human comfort is given priority. On some level, this essential manner of existence encourages critical thought.

In truth, life often presents us with far more complex issues than simply choosing what to dress. Cultivating critical thinking and reasoning abilities is crucial to address environmental problems. Reasoning offers several advantages that will enrich the African soil and encourage success. Progress will rule the day if Africans demonstrate superior deductive reasoning abilities and use critical thought to rule out false identities in their surroundings. There are several components to reasoning, including the capacity to hear and analyse information, patience and consistency, ownership of one's duties, open-mindedness, identity understanding, and attention, among others. One of the most significant issues in Africa is that most people there lack the motivation to learn about their past to understand their identity better. Good treatment of oneself is difficult if one does not understand who they are. When a religious leader wants to explain what God can accomplish for you, he will first explain who God is. Think about the following example: If a scientist decides to educate one on the function of a tissue, he will first inform you about what tissue is comprised of. A philosopher will also teach his students the fundamentals of philosophy before forcing them to appreciate its illusions and applicability. In the same vein, Africans should be concerned about their identity. Africans can reach this conclusion about knowing who they are, accepting who they are, and learning what they are capable of through reasoning. Suppose acceptance and appreciation of their identity are developed and held in high regard. In that case, it will build generational riches instead of some Africans rejecting to know and accept their identity and not being proud as Africans. Without any negativity to lessen the intensity of the thought process, this will foster unity and powerfully develop thoughts. As a result, the African community will be better able to put morality and duty ahead of feelings.

Africa has a long history of suffering under various heinous forms of slavery. Even most Africans think colonialism is to blame for their continent's underdevelopment. Subjectively speaking, it has been many years since slavery was abolished in Africa, yet the continent has not yet achieved grandeur, even though some would contend that slavery was improved to include mental servitude. If so, then figuring out a problem is also a solution component. If some Africans conclude that slavery has been upgraded to mental servitude, this insight should result in the abolition of misery and suffering in Africa. Sadly, Africa hasn't managed to shake off its undeveloped status yet. Does that imply that we may not be reasoning or thinking critically enough?

At this point, it will be crucial that Africans inspire themselves with strong feelings and mental images gleaned from history to reason based on conclusions made from evidence on our issues, setbacks, and unsuccessful strategies over the years. Instead of placing coffins on African soil or assigning blame to our ancestors, the problems in Africa need to be addressed with a solution spectacle. In addition, unity must be established via reason and critical thinking without division or bias to pave the way for African achievement. Even though thinking is about discovering truth and making better judgments, biases can occasionally be a factor. For instance, when one conducts incorrect research, they frequently reach the result they initially desired. Confirmation bias is the term for this. Due to the propensity to actively seek knowledge and prioritise data that supports one's preexisting beliefs over developing a balanced mental environment to consider new findings, this bias frequently results in poor conclusions. Reasoning is a collective activity, according to the social theory of reasoning. If two people researched the same discipline, they would present their findings and arguments for accuracy.

Confirmation bias is, therefore, more likely to diminish to the bare minimum and improve the cognitive job needed. The above analogy explains why Africa must work together to solve its poverty. The African community can choose what they want and how to communicate it rationally. The capacity for asking the proper questions and expressing desires is crucial for self-development. When the mind deviates from what it can conceive and what time can accommodate, one will likely ask incorrect questions (questions that cannot be answered on its terms but only dissolved by understanding the cognitive algorithm that births the awareness of a question). The wrong questions frequently result in short-term thinking and stagnation near the centre of one's expectations and drive for achievement. If one wishes to develop an infrastructure, for instance, and determines that there isn't enough money available, at what point can the infrastructure be built? Or you decide it's not possible, in which case you generate a want for something on one level and a desire to give up on that desire on another level. This uncertainty leads to a psychological conflict that may prevent the desire for it to happen.

The correct query should be, "How do we make it happen?" With logic and critical thinking, one understands that nature deals with what is and is not feasible, whereas one's business is to strive. Focus, a thinking component, is crucial to achieving tremendous success in one's life and society. As one of the wealthiest Americans in history and the driving force behind the growth of the American steel industry in the late 19th century, Scottish-American entrepreneur and philanthropist Andrew Carnegie discusses the key to his success. Andrew Carnegie claims to be able to focus on one item for five minutes at a time. In contrast, a bird family like the eagle can focus on a target or prey item and go for it despite any available barriers. Good decisions are made when critical thinking and reasoning are prioritised in daily life.

People Matters defines critical thinking as the capacity to make judgments and conclusions based on facts and logic while excluding feelings to enable the review and development of one's thought process. Moreover, to explore more in-depth potential solutions and outcomes based on evidence, critical thinking enables one to challenge all likely conclusions and results of arguments. In other words, someone who asks how, why, and when questions may end up on the path of critical thought. These kinds of inquiries help one arrive at wise judgments and choices. Different solutions to Africa's challenges will emerge from critical thinking and reasoning rather than the currently used tried-and-failed method. When Africans develop their critical thinking and reasoning abilities, they may eliminate the economic and social problems threatening the continent's future. By doing this, they can reduce the possibility of making rash decisions that will worsen their problems. Critical thinking and reasoning skills force one to ask questions to find the roots of decisions based on facts, evidence, or logical reasoning to attain success in the end.

Critical thinking and reasoning also help one become accountable for choices and behaviours. For instance, a person who commits manslaughter faces less severe punishment than someone who commits murder. The difference is that while both crimes are illegal and punishable, manslaughter is the inadvertent killing of another person, whereas murder is the intentional killing of a person. Murderers are always held accountable, arguably without mercy, and must face the justice of the law. Murder is frequently considered the most serious crime because it requires significant thinking and reasoning. In the school of life, taking ownership of one's successes and failures promotes progress, and making conscious decisions puts one in charge of the consequences.

In order to find the best answer to an issue, claim, question, or circumstance, critical thinking is used in such scenarios. You must base your decisions on facts, evidence, and logical conclusions if you want to use your reasoning skills, which go hand in hand with critical thinking. An individual can analyse information and generate an unbiased opinion using critical thinking. You can arrive at reasonable findings by objectively assessing the relevant information to aid your decision-making. Critical thinking is evaluating information objectively and reaching a reasoned conclusion.

It also requires gathering information about a subject and utilising deductive reasoning to discern between information pertaining to the issue and information not. Since critical thinking abilities benefit people personally and professionally, most firms promote them. Critical thinking skills are a fantastic benefit for employment since employers reward those who can effectively assess a situation and come up with a reasoned answer. Since time is a valuable resource for the majority of managers, they will benefit significantly from a worker who can make wise judgments on their own.

Analysing information accurately is the most essential aspect of critical thinking. Having the ability to analyse information requires the ability to gather, comprehend, and evaluate data. When studying a job issue, analytical thinking helps separate information that applies to your situation from information that does not. Effective communication is crucial to the critical thinking process, whether you use it to gather data or convince others that your conclusions are correct. Sharing information and ideas with others and showcasing your capacity for critical thought are requirements for success. Being in close contact with your coworkers can help you gather the information you need to make the best decision while choosing a job. Finding particular patterns in data and making abstract connections between seemingly unrelated pieces of information will help your critical thinking develop. By critically analysing a job technique or procedure, you can cleverly come up with strategies to make it more efficient and quick. Creativity is valued across all professions, levels of experience, and industries as a skill that can be improved over time. Their primary education and life experiences influence a person's ability to evaluate certain circumstances objectively. By being conscious of these biases, you can improve your general decision-making and critical thinking skills. For example, if you have a specific meeting strategy, but your partner suggests a different approach, you should let them speak and adjust your plan in light of what they say. Another essential skill is the ability to effectively analyse a problem and work toward discovering a solution. For instance, if your restaurant's waitstaff needs to enhance service rates, you can consider delegating some of their duties to bussers or other kitchen staff so the servers can bring food more quickly. Asking the proper questions is essential to come to the correct conclusions in both personal and professional contexts.

When you think that the knowledge and skills of another person could make your work more effective, think about asking outcome-based questions. By asking someone how they would react in a hypothetical situation, you can uncover new viewpoints and learn about their capacity for critical thought. When you think that the knowledge and skills of another person could make your work more effective, think about asking outcome-based questions. By asking someone how they would react in a hypothetical situation, you can uncover new viewpoints and learn about their capacity for critical thought. You can get insight by asking someone to consider, assess, and describe their mental processes surrounding an experience. By using examples from the real world, this strategy can aid in the development of critical thinking. Asking how something works is a simple technique to gain an understanding of something. Any functioning system is the result of a protracted process of trial and error, and being fully aware of the processes required to achieve success could make you more effective in your endeavours.

Critical thinkers have particular characteristics that enable them to think in this way. While some people are born with certain traits, others must actively work on them. Open-mindedness, respect for logic and evidence, the ability to take into account other viewpoints and perspectives—or, to put it another way, cognitive flexibility, the ability to move around from one position to another—scepticism, clarity, and precision are few of the dispositions. Good critical thinkers must present compelling cases. Making a claim and providing evidence to back it up is an argument. In a productive conflict, it's critical to use well-considered arguments. It would help to mentally consider several arguments to conclude when critically analysing a situation. Critical thinking necessitates deducing conclusions in addition to discussions. You must be able to reason to draw logical conclusions from the information and arguments offered. This conclusion will decide the optimum line of action. Distinguishing fact from fiction can occasionally be a part of critical thinking. You might not always encounter equally valid arguments. A critical thinker must recognise that certain conditions must be satisfied before something can be considered believable. The capacity to reflect on one's own thinking is known as metacognition. Critical thinkers should be able to evaluate their own ideas to determine whether or not they have considered all possible outcomes. Its outcome aids them in developing more accurate hypotheses.

Critical thinking soft skills support critical thinking, according to the definition. Your capacity to think critically can be enhanced by developing these abilities. The ability to think critically is seen as one of several transferable abilities in the workplace. Many of these are soft talents that can be applied in different contexts. According to data by America Succeeds, critical thinking is among the top five most frequently requested lasting skills in job ads. The top five permanent talents are sought 2.6 times more often than the top five hard skills. These results demonstrate the need for soft skills like critical thinking in the workplace. For instance, the majority of the time, working as an accountant can be simple. But critical thinking abilities can be necessary. What happens, for instance, if some expenses are difficult to divide into straightforward categories? An accountant will find it difficult to work independently and solve problems alone if they lack critical thinking abilities. Critical thinking skills are essential in daily life as well. You can analyse several potential fixes for issues at home by having a solid basis for critical thinking. Additionally, it can help you analyse several points of view, create the best answer for challenging problems, and improve your learning.

The fifth aspect of critical thinking, metacognition, depends on this critical thinking ability. It entails being aware of your own cognitive biases as well as those of others. Biases can affect how someone interprets the information that is given to them. However, if you're conscious of your biases, you may challenge yourself and take into account alternative viewpoints. It's crucial to recognise biases, especially for hiring decision-makers. This is because, if left unchecked, biases against particular minority groups might result in workplace disparities. Think of a hiring manager who is comparing two resumes. Their instinct may cause them to reject one of the resumes because of bias against the other gender. Imagine, however, that the hiring manager learns about their bias. They could next ponder whether or not this bias is affecting their judgment.

The capacity to make inferences with thorough scrutiny, which is unbiased and based on available information, is essential in such scenarios. Without inference, taking action after analysing the relevant data can be challenging. Being able to process information is essential for making thoughtful decisions. For illustration, let's return to the accountant having trouble categorising a business expense properly. They can evaluate other comparable circumstances and extrapolate the most logical categorisation from that data. Discovering the facts is necessary before analysing the data and drawing a judgment. Finding data to support your arguments requires research abilities. You won't always have access to the necessary information. You must have research abilities to delve into a situation and obtain the data you need to analyse critically. Some situations don't call for more investigation. For instance, a first responder who arrives at the site of a vehicle accident won't do additional investigation. They must evaluate what they see before them to determine which injuries require immediate medical attention.

On the other hand, a person conducting a market analysis will need to investigate competitors and compile data before forming an opinion. When compared to inference and research, identification is distinct. It requires the ability to recognise an issue as well as the factors that are influencing it. In other words, it takes identification for someone to realise that they need to approach anything critically. It will be tough for someone to recognise when to analyse a scenario without the right identifying abilities. As an example, let's consider the situation of entering data into a spreadsheet. Not, as usual, the statistics aren't showing up. It would be simple to continue without comprehending a problem's root cause if one could not recognise difficulties. But as soon as you understand what's happening, you can see that the spreadsheet's methodology is flawed. Once you realise the technique is flawed, you can only start investigating what's happening to identify a fix. Never be afraid to disprove conventional wisdom and learn more about interesting subjects. Intellectual curiosity is a valuable skill, particularly for critical thinking. One way to foster curiosity is to adopt a beginner's mindset. You may keep an open mind if you look at every problem from a beginner's point of view. You might not be able to perceive certain things if your mind is not ready for assessment. Not all information is relevant in the same way. Making a critical judgment requires evaluating the information's relevance. Consider fundamental online research techniques. You have access to a wealth of knowledge on almost any subject imaginable. However, when conducting research online, you must continuously determine whether what you see is relevant. Without applying relevance judgment, you would squander too much time on activities that wouldn't substantially impact the target aim. You might give that information more weight if you can pinpoint what's most crucial.

Take charge of the software quality assurance (QA) team. However, because the spreadsheet used for the regression must be manually filled out, it creates a bottleneck whenever your team wants to input a bug. To function efficiently, your group requires you to do this duty. This procedure takes place once a week and costs each team member 30 minutes. It would be better to figure out what is going on initially. The team is confined because you are the team leader and have access to the information required to finish the regression spreadsheet. After then, you can look up information. You can ask higher-ups why you are the only one with access to this data.

You may also ask other teams for suggestions on possible solutions to this problem. After making your inquiry, analyse the facts to determine the information's applicability. That information is no longer relevant because you cannot use the solutions developed by some teams. Before you analyse your data, check whether you have any personal biases. For instance, you might not get along with one of the other team leads. Therefore, you might decide to disregard the details they have offered. You can, however, put aside your preconceived thoughts about this person and acknowledge the worth of their answer by acknowledging this prejudice. After you've analysed, it's time to develop a creative solution. You understand that your team will benefit from time savings by creating an automated script. And it will do it without consuming excessive resources from the engineering department. Present your remedy to your manager next. Describe how you arrived at this decision. Suppose your spreadsheet automation approach has been approved. Looking back and assessing what happens after using the solution is necessary. Wait until the spreadsheet has accumulated enough information and has been used for a while. Here is one example. It was evident that the bottleneck had been fixed due to the remedy. The script, however, makes the spreadsheet sluggish and challenging to use. You would have to start the process from the beginning and go back to the drawing board.

Generally, one can improve their critical thinking skills with these techniques:

- Play games that require critical thinking skills

- Ask more questions, even basic ones

- Question your assumptions

- Develop your technical skills so that you can identify problems more efficiently.

- Find ways to solve more problems (at work and home)

- Become aware of your mental processes, like the availability heuristic

- Think for yourself: don't adopt other people's opinions without questioning them first

- Seek out the diversity of thought

- Start developing foresight

- Try active listening

- Weigh the consequences of different actions before you act

- Seek a mentor who can help you develop these skills

- Get professional coaching.

DISCIPLINE

Discipline. Thousands of thoughts on one word. Is it a penalty? Is it a submission? Are they laws? Is it an application? Does it consistently act in the same way? Is it consistently doing morally? Is it dependable? Does it carry out your instructions? Is it stiff? Is it dull? Do you have a choice at all? Do you just acquiesce? Let's examine the word's origin to determine its meaning and proper usage in order to comprehend what discipline is and what it signifies. The word "disciple," the basis for the concept of discipline, derives from the Latin word discipulus, which means "student." Because of the religious context, most people mistakenly think that a disciple is a "follower," although the actual meaning of the word is "student," as in "one who studies." The word "discipline" is derived from the Latin word "discipline," which means "instruction and training." It comes from the Latin word discere, which means "to learn."

What, therefore, is discipline? A standards system is studied, learned, practiced, and applied in the discipline. Discipline is different from rules, regulations, or punishment. It is not submission, enforcement, or conformity. It isn't rigid, repetitive, or marked by much repetition. No such thing as eternal punishment exists. You perform it for your own gain. Even though you might get guidance or instruction from one or more sources, discipline comes from inside. It is there. Following someone else's rules in order to avoid punishment does not constitute discipline. Achieving significant objectives requires learning and applying deliberate actions. You have the decision to be disciplined. It is a choice. Even better, all of your choices. Distinguishing between discipline as an internal or external dynamic, a law or a deliberate choice, is essential. Your gateway to a better, more discipline-driven living is a deeper understanding of this. Do you understand how it works? When you view discipline as a choice you make, not someone else's or anything else's, you have control. Greater discretion, choice, and discipline. Less control, fewer options, and less self-discipline.

Moreover, let's use a typical example. "I want to get up at 4:45 am and work out. My four-month-old baby wakes up at 6:00 in the morning and, like many babies, requires much time and care. By 7:30 am, I had to take care of him, make coffee, get ready, and head to work. I set my alarm for 4:45 am because I need to exercise before he gets up. When my alarm goes off, I decide to be disciplined and get up to work out before waking up and lovingly waking up my son. My first victory of the day is in the books, and now that my workout is over and I don't need to "find the time" to make it up later, my mind is free to concentrate on my next objectives. I am in charge of my day and myself. I can even consume a little at lunch or dinner because I worked out hard. I burned, so I earned. Notwithstanding, what if I don't choose discipline?

My alarm goes off; I decide to sleep instead, wake up my son, still show him love, and go to work. I should have woken up and worked out. Therefore, I'm upset psychologically and emotionally. I'm trying to think of when I can make it up. Tonight? Too busy, late, and worn out. Tomorrow? I was meant to have the day off. I'm now discouraged and preoccupied. I have no control over my day or myself. I already have a bad day, so my self-control further deteriorates because I'm stressed out and upset, and I make impulsive food choices at lunch and supper. It could as well have followed a pattern.

Right, it sounds familiar. The two possibilities mentioned above apply to every situation in any setting. We retain control of ourselves and how we move through our circumstances when we preserve our discipline and freedom of choice. When we renounce discipline and free will, we cede power to other people, outside forces, and the unavoidable randomness of life. We drift and become the plaything of circumstances (Frankl, V. E. (1992). So, more discipline, more choice, more control. Better options. Higher standards. Improved skill. More flexibility. Less discipline, less choice, less control. Fewer options. Lower standards. Inadequate skill. Less flexibility.

As mentioned, learning to lead yourself effectively and others comes down to discipline. Focus and self-control lead to fulfilment, happiness, and success. When faced with an all-you-can-eat buffet, the chance to make quick cash or the sleepy allure of staying in rather than joining the Peloton, it may not be easy to believe, but studies show that those with self-discipline are happier. Why? Because when we exercise self-control and discipline, we achieve more of the objectives that are most important to us. The link between setting goals and goals achieved is self-discipline. As Plato rightly said, "The first and best victory is to conquer self." Self-control experts spend less time debating whether to engage in actions and behaviours inconsistent with their values or objectives. They make better decisions. They resist letting emotions or impulses guide their decisions. They are the designers of their ideas and the steps they take to achieve the desired result. As a result, they are less susceptible to being side-tracked by temptation and exhibit higher levels of life satisfaction. "You have power over your mind—not outside events. Realise this, and you will find strength." (Aurelius.M, AD121). There are specific strategies one can execute to learn self-discipline and acquire the willpower to live a happier, more fulfilling life.

Nonetheless, know your strengths and weaknesses. Everybody has weaknesses. They all have a similar impact on us, whether it is the urge for alcohol, tobacco, unhealthy food, a preoccupation with social media, or the video game Fortnite (by the way, what the heck is with this game?!). However, weaknesses are not limited to instances in which we lack self-control. Each of us has areas where we excel, as well as areas where we kind of fail. For example, I don't particularly appreciate keeping my temper when someone is shooting at me, lengthy paperwork that requires searching through old files I never preserved, having difficult talks, and using automated phone systems. So I used to steer clear of these things actively (or consciously). I now try to confront them head-on—or delegate them to others. Self-awareness is vital for comfort zone expansion; however, constant focus and acknowledging your shortcomings is a substantial orientation. Too frequently, people either attempt to deny the existence of their vulnerabilities or, with a rigid mindset, give in to them, throwing up their hands in despair and saying, "Oh well." Recognise your advantages, but more importantly, accept your weaknesses. Until you do, you cannot triumph over them.

Oscar Wilde said, "I can resist anything except temptation." Out of sight, out of mind, as the saying goes. Although it may sound absurd, this saying offers wise counsel. You can dramatically increase your self-control by eliminating the immense temptations from your surroundings. My entire life had to alter when I pursued my dream of becoming a seal. Throw the fast food away if you want to eat healthy. Want to consume less alcohol? Get rid of the alcohol. Turn off social media notifications, silence your phone, and organise your to-do list better to increase your productivity at work. Set goals and carry them out. The fewer distractions one has, the more focused one will be on accomplishing one goal. Set yourself up for success by ditching bad influences.

Similarly, like any objective, if you want to develop better self-discipline, you must know what you want to achieve. Also, you need to know what success means to you. After all, it's simple to become lost or diverted if you don't know where you're heading. Always prioritise. Each time-limited step you need to take to accomplish your goals is laid out in a clear strategy. Make up a mantra to help you stay concentrated. Successful people use this method to stay on course, feel emotionally invested in their objective, and define a distinct finish line. Correspondingly, self-control is a learned behaviour; it is not something we are born with. It also needs regular repetition and practice to be mastered, just like any other talent. That must become second nature. Self-discipline calls for effort and concentration, which can be exhausting. Maintaining your willpower as time passes can get harder and harder. It can feel harder to do other duties that require restraint the stronger the temptation or decision is. Thus, work on developing self-discipline by being diligent daily in areas related to a goal. It would help if you had a plan to exercise everyday diligence. Whichever works best for you, put it on your calendar, to-do list, or even as a tattoo on the back of your eyelids. Anybody may regularly stretch the limits of their comfort zone with practice.

Subsequently, developing self-control and establishing a new habit can initially seem overwhelming, mainly if you concentrate on the entire task. Keep things basic so that you won't feel intimidated. Make your objective into manageable, little steps. Focus on performing one thing consistently and develop self-discipline with that objective in mind rather than trying to alter everything at once. As they say in the SEAL Teams, "Eat the elephant one bite at a time." Start by working out for ten or fifteen minutes each day if you're attempting to lose weight but don't exercise frequently (or at all). Start by going to bed 30 minutes earlier each night to develop improved sleeping habits. Change your grocery shopping routine and start meal prepping if you want to eat healthier. Take it slow. You can eventually add more objectives to your list as your thinking and behaviour change. Also, you won't likely go beyond your willpower's boundaries if you think it is finite. Studies demonstrate that willpower can wane over time, as I already said. But what if that impression were to change? As we adopt the concept of willpower without restrictions, we continue to advance, accomplish more, and strengthen our mental fortitude. It follows the same principles as "stretch" goals. In other words, our internal ideas about self-control and willpower can influence our discipline. You'll offer a greater incentive to achieve those goals if you can eliminate these ingrained barriers and have faith in your journey to success.

Likewise, implementation intention is a method that psychologists employ to strengthen willpower. That's when you make a strategy for handling a potentially challenging issue you'll most likely encounter. To be clear, I'm not talking about a contingency plan that assumes you'll probably fail at Plan A. Imagine you want to master the trapeze but tell yourself you won't be very good at it, so you'll probably stick with miniature golf instead. That is a mediocre backup strategy wrapped in a lame one. Not preparing for failure, but rather provisions for deliberate course modification. Be courageous and keep going on. A strategy can help you approach the circumstance with the mindset and restraint required. You will also conserve energy by avoiding needing to make an instant judgment based on your emotions. Coaches who are capable of providing constructive, sometimes harsh feedback are essential for the development of expertise. True experts are highly motivated students seeking this kind of criticism. They are also adept at recognising when and if the guidance of a coach or mentor doesn't work for them. The top achievers I've known and collaborated with were always aware of their positive behaviours while focusing on their negative ones. They purposefully chose impersonal trainers who would push them and encourage them to perform at higher levels. The top coaches can help you prepare by pointing out areas of your performance that need to be improved for your next level of competence.

Occasionally, despite our best efforts and carefully thought-out plans, we fall short. There will be highs and lows, spectacular accomplishments and terrible tragedies. Never giving up is the key. If you become stuck, use the five WHYs to determine the root cause before moving forward. It's best not to let guilt, fury, or frustration overwhelm you because doing so will only make you feel worse and keep you from progressing. Recognise your shortcomings and extend forgiveness to yourself. Then return your attention to the game and play harshly. Building discipline is a practice, not a destination or standard. Even though practice never ends, we get better at what we do. Many people try to be disciplined, yet it's more complicated than we think to become disciplined. Our mental health, upbringing, personal habits, and current situations influence our ability to handle ourselves. Like self-love or addressing our anxieties requires careful effort, learning to be disciplined does too. Even though it can appear to be an insurmountable dragon, improvement is always attainable. You may acquire the self-discipline that matters for you and your goals through practice by learning to work within the constraints of who you are and what you have. Beating ourselves up or comparing our "lack" of self-discipline to others doesn't help. Instead of thinking about self-discipline as a personality attribute, give up that idea and concentrate on using it to help you live the life you want.

Evidence illustrates that life without discipline is like a ship without a rudder. No man or woman who lacks self-discipline has ever developed an influential personality. Such discipline must be focused on the formation of resolutely good character rather than acting as a means in and of itself. Discipline's key is motivation. Men who are adequately driven will exercise discipline on their own. It is better to be cut up and burned than nurtured to grow. Discipline is the skeleton that gives a person structure and protection if love is the person's heart. Sometimes learning from mistakes and failures is a discipline in itself. Discipline is most effective when used to educate internal controls. Keep your composure when circumstances are difficult. Making oneself a master in any endeavour is, in my opinion, the key to outstanding achievement. The basic discipline is one of self-control.

Daily small disciplines practised result in tremendous accomplishments attained gradually over time. What is within our power to do, lies within our power not to do; the most powerful has himself in his power. Discipline is the link between goals and accomplishments. Therefore, there isn't a magic wand that can address all of our issues. Our effort and discipline must be used to find a solution. You will never have more or less control over yourself than that. A man's level of success is determined by how well he controls himself; his level of failure is determined by how well he abandons himself. Additionally, this law is a manifestation of eternal justice. He will not have control over others if he cannot achieve dominance over himself.

DEDICATION

The solution to almost all issues in life is dedication. Dedication can imply many things, but they all show a single-minded devotion to anything in life. A person is said to be dedicated to something if they will do anything for it, no matter what, and without looking back. For instance, you enjoy creating flower gardens. Now, for that to happen, you'll need a few things. You will need to put in much effort and time while being committed. After all, your main objective is to create a garden filled with various lovely plants. As a result, your constancy in investing time and effort will be referred to as your dedication. We've all heard the saying that strenuous effort and dedication go hand in hand, or that, in the words of Vince Lombardi, a great American football player and coach, "hard labour and dedication to the job at hand" are the price of success. Dedication encompasses all of these and more. A successful life results from arduous effort and dedication; life is about commitment to a desired outcome, a goal you can't shake. It's one thing to devote yourself to your profession, but what does it mean to devote oneself so entirely that it consumes all your thoughts daily? When you don't know where to begin, how can you dedicate yourself to your objectives to attain the most remarkable success? Being entirely dedicated to something, whether it be something tangible like a task, objective, or desired result, or something you can physically feel yourself being a part of, like a cause, religion, sports team, or another person, is the act of dedication. While there are many kinds of dedication, I will concentrate on what it means to devote oneself to a purpose—your genuine calling, if you will—in this piece. A strong character quality that will most likely help you succeed in life is dedication. Commitment, devotion, adherence, allegiance, single-mindedness, purposefulness, and doggedness are just a few of the words (synonyms) for dedication.

Although they are synonyms, these words cannot always be used interchangeably. Thus, I have chosen to use "dedication" throughout this article. Starting with the goal entails having a distinct concept of your final destination. In order to better comprehend where you are right now and ensure that the steps you take are always in the proper direction, it means knowing where you're headed. To truly dedicate oneself to your goals, you must begin with the end in mind and look backward. This level of commitment necessitates that you visualise reaching your objectives in the future and scheduling your most necessary chores first to get there, ahead of all other, less crucial ones. Start at the finish line rather than the beginning of your journey to achieve your goals. What action did you take in the closing moments before completing the task? What was the step that came before that, the step before that, and the step before that?

Reverse-engineering the processes to attain your goals gives you the impression that you are finally in control. Still, the only way to get back to where you started is to travel all the way home in reverse and accelerate more quickly when you get there.

The secret is to schedule your priorities rather than prioritise what is on your agenda. That isn't a deep thought, is it? Similarly, Shane Parrish, the creator of Farnam Street, recently said, "Don't tell me your priorities. I want to see your calendar. When they are planned, your priorities cannot slip through the cracks. Despite your best intentions, we both know it's unlikely to happen if you don't schedule time to complete your goals throughout the upcoming week. While setting your priorities is one way to commit yourself to success, it's necessary to ensure you're consistently working on the most important components of your goals. One of the most potent tools we have for reshaping our lives and achieving our objectives is dedication. Committing and devotion will develop your work ethic, and you'll stand out. Workplace dedication and devotion can be seen in various ways, including putting in extra hours, suggesting solutions that will benefit the company, helping your coworkers, keeping a positive attitude, and being on time.

Committing to your job need not indicate that you want to spend the rest of your life there. Consider seasonal workers who can be dedicated to their profession throughout their little period, such as instructors seeking employment in the summer or farmers augmenting their income in the winter. Only variables based on performance and work ethics are important. There are practical talents you can add to your resume and master at work to catch your employer's eye, regardless of whether you're employed temporarily, full-time, or in an "I'll have to wait and see how this pans out" kind of employment (in a good way).

In a job setting, for instance, when you continually desire to learn new things, it shows that you are committed to executing your work as best as possible. Also, it demonstrates your concern for both your development and the prosperity of the business. Examples of proactive learning include:

•   Asking inquiries both to your own department and to other departments.

•   Enrolling in online classes and seminars.

•   Updating yourself on developments in your field.

•   Attempting to earn a qualification or accolade.

•   Volunteering to help with tasks outside of your area of expertise will provide you with more practical experience.

Work extra hours. Even if it's not always the most enjoyable thing, it demonstrates to your employer that you are a go-getter willing to put in the additional time. Giving time to your job is the best way to show commitment. Remember that some employers won't let you work overtime unless a significant project or deadline is approaching and that you don't want to exhaust yourself too quickly by giving up all control of your work-life balance. Working overtime includes coming in early, remaining late, or being available round-the-clock for emergencies or client questions after business hours.

Pitch ideas that will help the company. Employees who are not engaged or intentionally disengaged are content to punch in, complete the bare minimum of work required while counting the hours until the end of the workday, and then punch out. They may be aware of ineffective procedures but lack the motivation to take action. They view those issues as being outside the scope of their responsibilities. By identifying problems at work and suggesting fixes, you can demonstrate your problem-solving abilities even if you are not in a managerial or supervisory position. This extra effort significantly strengthens your commitment by showing that you care. Citing concrete instances of how you increased your previous company's productivity is a great highlight on your resume if you decide to leave your position. Help your team. "Teamwork makes the dream work," as the phrase goes. Businesses don't succeed on the backs of lone employees; it takes a team to accomplish goals. By devoting your time and talents to assisting your coworkers, you're demonstrating your commitment to the firm's success. Examples of assisting your team include:

- Offering to mentor new hires.

- Assisting a coworker to complete a significant project on time.

- Mentioning a resource you found useful.

Have a positive outlook. It's obvious when you're content and motivated. Concentrating on the positives may encourage your coworkers to do the same and make a strong impression on clients. Employees who are highly motivated to develop and achieve goals most times exhibit positivity as a critical quality. Keeping a positive outlook involves, among other things, not criticising your employer, coworkers, or clients, as well as approaching problems with an "I can do this" attitude. Bringing a professional attitude to work and leaving personal problems at the door; keeping a composed, patient, and upbeat demeanour when dealing with irate consumers.

Again, Be on time. Being on time for work alone reveals a lot about a person. It conveys to your company and coworkers that you value their time and one's own time while also demonstrating consideration for them. Being punctual also demonstrates other soft skills that employers value, such as time management and organisational habits (you probably aren't always on time if you frequently forget your keys or to get lunch), as well as the ability to prepare by being prepared for bad weather or construction delays. Being punctual also demonstrates other soft skills that employers value, such as time management and organisational habits (you probably aren't always on time if you frequently forget your keys or to get lunch), as well as the ability to prepare by being prepared for bad weather or construction delays. The value of dedication is found in its capacity to inspire perseverance through even the most difficult tasks or jobs. If you are dedicated to it, you will always find a reason to continue your current action. If you keep looking for reasons to move forward, you will succeed.

Let's consider this from the viewpoint below. For your relationship to last, you must be committed to one another. After all, being committed to someone means you won't ever consider loving or cherishing anyone else while focused on that person. The same is true of your attempts in life. Being entirely focused and committed to whatever task you are working on will enable you to finish it. Therefore, dedication becomes crucial in what you do. It will be harder for you to finish what you've started or even do well at it if you somehow think about doing other things while engaging in other activities that are wholly unrelated to your primary activity. In that regard, commitment is crucial because it enables you to finish what you've started. It's comparable to how a relationship will only endure for a long time if both parties are fully dedicated.

Hence, no matter how long it takes to complete a task you started for your reasons, you must commit to it and be wholly devoted to it. Because being committed to your goal or objective enables you to stay the course and complete it, devotion is crucial in all areas of life. Committing to something indicates that you will remain with it no matter what and persevere through challenges. Disadvantages will be surmounted until the objective is attained, leading to success with dedication and perseverance. Because Rome wasn't constructed in a single day, success didn't happen overnight. You must put forth much effort and take all necessary measures to succeed. Hence commitment is essential for success.

Finally, with hard work and dedication, anything is possible. Any site worth visiting has no shortcuts. Happiness is attainable via dedication. It aids in removing any fears. If you're a student, your life's goal is to read and succeed academically. Your dedication will help your consistency with your goal. If you lack dedication, you will abandon your aim too quickly. It's easy. Being dedicated is a virtue. You have to learn to be dedicated to being successful in life. Dedication is like being sincere and honest about a particular aim in life. Love your dream and passion for being dedicated. It will only make your life simple.

CHAPTER 5

MEASURES AND MODELS THAT CAN DEVELOP AFRICA

The African continent's economy is still underdeveloped after years of conceptualizing, creating, and implementing numerous economic policies and programs. Most of the world's poor live in this area but have little control over allocating resources. Africa's development challenges exceed its low income, dwindling trade shares, limited savings, and slow growth. The HIV/AIDS pandemic, severe inequality, unequal access to resources, stigmatisation, instability, and environmental damage are some further examples.

The underdevelopment of Africa has been addressed in the past through various tactics. Others include the 1980 Lagos Action Plan, the ECA Alternative Structural Adjustment Programme for Africa, and the African Scope of Reference for SAPS for Socio-Economic Redressing and Transformation, in addition to the complementary UN Programme for the Economic Redress and Development of Africa and the 1986-1990 Priority Programme for Economic Redressing of Africa (PPREA), which was adopted by the OAU in 1985. These efforts haven't been implemented in full. The New Partnership for African Development (NEPAD) is the newest initiative. This initiative combines the Millennium Action Plan for African Recovery initiative (MAP), the New Compact with Africa, and the Omega Plan. It represents a further step toward enshrining development in African leaders' collective commitment and vision. The long-term goal is to put African nations on the road toward sustainable development, to stop the continent's marginalisation in the process of globalisation and to help them navigate the challenges of the twenty-first century by attaining their growth.

No section of the world has not suffered conflict, yet Africa continues to be a hotbed of political unrest and economic hardship. In contrast, other regions have made progress in these areas. Several factors contribute to the current state of poverty in Africa, including political, social and economic factors. The number and intensity of the conflicts have risen because of the increased liberalisation and growth of international trade that followed the end of the Cold War. Conflicts frequently result from a combination of generic label governance, the multiethnic makeup of the states, and the circumstances surrounding their declaration of independence. The winds of change had pushed for a democratic administration in Africa. Africa had seen pressure for the democratic government from the wind of change. Unfortunately, some of the process's leaders were already in place and switched to the Democratic Party out of convenience rather than genuine conviction. The facts mentioned above demonstrated the true causes of Africa's underdevelopment. Over the past forty years, Africa has benefited from various developmental programs - from domestic and international actors. Many of the issues that Africa is currently facing, like the debt crisis, extreme poverty and political instability, to name a few, are regrettably the result of these endeavours, according to several development professionals. While there are many other theories and methods for expanding Africa's economy, the major kwarternational donors' promotion of the mainstream development discourse has centred on the requirement for economic growth to achieve sustainable development.

The primary goal of this write-up is to provide models or metrics for the growth of the African continent. First, this write-up broadens the criteria for African development and centres on four issues Africa should pursue to further its development. The first theme emphasises how political stability within the continent can promote peace, stimulating development and economic growth. The second theme is governance, specifically in terms of solid leadership and level of development. This theme will focus on the relationship between economic transformation, peace and good governance as a precondition for development since a peaceful environment encourages economic transformation, good resource and asset management, income mobilisation and a state of progress. It will also show how peace combined with good governance and a state of development would enable economic transformation, this being an additional incentive for economic growth in Africa. The third theme aims to clarify why economic expansion is essential for Africa's development. However, economic progress and liberalisation have been hailed as the best chance for global wealth and the modern development of Africa. As is demonstrated by the current globalisation era, in which the continent will mobilise its resources, particularly in terms of dynamic sectors of development, exploit the advantages of international trade and liberalise the market, whereby the continent is required to design its policies to meet the demands of the global market because individual governments are unable to carry out the market competition in the globalised order. The final theme, albeit not the final one, focuses on globalisation, a global network of interdependence. According to this viewpoint, the continent needs stability, strong leadership and economic transformation to be prepared to take advantage of the benefits of globalisation through interdependence among nations.

Additionally, good governance and democratisation of service would encourage accountability and responsiveness to people's needs. They would make it easier to plan for the future and demonstrate its link to economic growth, resulting in genuine continental development. By utilising the qualifications mentioned above, this write-up will conclude by offering suggestions and recommendations on how the African continent could succeed in development. The growth and success of Africa in the twenty-first century would result from the union of all these four factors.

Peace and security are first. Peace is not commonly considered a result of development, either in development theory or development discourse. In searching for alternative development strategies in postcolonial Africa, internal and external security should be important considerations. During internal political terror in Africa since the Cold War is partially to blame for the continent's development halt, it is vital to consider both development and security. Political terror has consistently damaged development and security, whilst development theory and discourse, ranging from modernisation theory to global neo-liberalism, have dominated developmental policies in Africa and generated an Africa devoid of development. Foreign-sponsored political terror, as evidenced by collateral damage, caused widespread fear and instability and struck the human resources, political institutions and economic order at the centre of progress. Although political terror in Africa has not ended with the conclusion of the Cold War, aspects of it need to be considered for the continent's alternative development strategy. Some of the characteristics include a decrease in foreign aid to Africa, disarmament and a revision of the intellectual underpinnings of the African state. This necessitates a change from a military state to a developmental state with citizen engagement in order to lessen internal strife and address the exterior challenges of the new post-Cold War global system. According to Himmelstrand (1994), development theory must consider African societies' unique context and history. Thus, the suggestions listed below are no panacea for every African country but rather a framework for dealing with development and security. Development programs must pursue peace prudently, as I will demonstrate in economic reconstruction.

Maloka (2002) acknowledges the contributions made by the Organisation of African Unity, the African Union, the New Economic Partnership for Africa's Development and other organisations that have worked to advance African peace and development since the continent's independence. Peace is the primary requirement for successful growth, as acknowledged by the G8 Gleneagles Communiqué on Africa in 2005. It supports Africa's efforts to create a stable and peaceful continent. It will assist Africa's vulnerable states in resolving their conflicts and crises. Following the UN Charter, it supports African activities to prevent, mediate, fix, and consolidate disputes. It recognises that peace is one of the prerequisites for development in African countries and that its existence and being experienced is a critical first step in rethinking development. Peace is one of the prerequisites for economic growth and development, and these thoughts add to our ability to rethink development.

Furthermore, since peace does not mean the military must be disbanded, defence operations must consider how they will affect sustainable development. Therefore, peace and security must function within the development context for progress. I have made an effort to prove that there is a link between peace and progress. Economic progress and development are hampered by political terrorism, which creates an unsettling sense of unease. An illustration of how

US proxy wars, civil wars and terrorism have destroyed political establishments, economic order, and human capital is the Cold War in Southern Africa. Therefore, disarmament and other peace-promoting activities must be included as prerequisites to growth when conceptualising the continent's development.

Additionally, consideration should be given to the demands of the Cold War on Africa and any future effects of 9/11. Foreign direct investment can take the form of a loan, grant or any other type of development aid given to poorer countries, as well as the purchase of company interests in another nation. Their fundamental feature, however, is that it provides the donor with governments or institutions some decision-making authority within the receiving country's economic (and occasionally political) context. According to this viewpoint, the African nations would take full advantage while respecting the conditions placed by donor powers.

The second theme is governance and leadership. Africans must be involved in the decision-making process if they are to support the program. Good administration boosts both democratic and economic efficiency. In order for Africans to own globalisation and actively participate in it, the principle mentioned above is essential inside each African nation. Every African country must make considerable investments in developing human capital as part of economic governance. In today's knowledge-based global economy, having a flexible, educated, and healthy workforce is crucial for progress. Investment in human capital promotes personal development and offers a means of escaping poverty. Greater financial support for human capital development should come from regional cooperation and the global community. The idea that growth is the result of ongoing technological innovation, industrial upgrading, diversified portfolios, and advancements in the various institutional and infrastructure arrangements that serve as the foundation for business growth and wealth creation, which can be summed up as economic structural transformation, is strongly emphasised in modern theories of economic expansion. The theories also emphasise that market mechanisms would not be sufficient and that the government could help companies deal with the numerous informational, coordinational, and externality problems that usually arise with modern economic growth. Recent research by young economists suggests that the state in Africa may be vital to economic diversification and structural change. Historical evidence shows that all countries that successfully made the transition from agricultural to modern, sophisticated economies had governments that took the initiative to assist private firms during their structural change to resolve coordination and externality difficulties. A wide range of factors and conditions, including knowledge and innovation, human capital, institutions, and physical amenities, as well as fiscal, monetary, exchange rate, capital flow, trade, and other policies, affect the effectiveness of such endeavours. Because of this, the state's critical role depends less on how much it participates in economic transformation and more on its ability to direct growth with a clear ideological emphasis, strong institutions, and policies supported by enough organisational and administrative capability and political will. In many African countries, the state has been unable to bring about meaningful structural changes to the economy. It is well known that many African nations have seen significant growth volatility as a result of incomplete structural change, leaving them vulnerable to normal fluctuations in the world commodities markets. Several interconnected factors cause this susceptibility to external shocks. The reallocation of production resources from less productive to more productive sectors in an effort to diversify African economies away from core commodity sectors and toward high-value-added industries and services has led to ineffective development strategies. Second, unbalanced incentives for economic reform and diversification have frequently been connected to several African countries' surplus of natural resources. Third, the continent's unfavourable geography and environment have to varying degrees harmed the continent's economic transformation. These factors present significant barriers to achieving higher labour productivity, limit access to sizable markets, limit economies of scale, drive up production costs, and result in low production efficiency. Fourth, Africa lags behind the rest of the world regarding infrastructural quality, political and economic institutions, and business environment. This problem is related to inadequate incentives for innovative long-term investment and private sector growth and ineffective systems for allocating resources. Additionally, it adds to the continent's underfunding of social programs and public services. Last but not least, many African countries struggle to maximise the potential of their citizens. As a result, little public ownership and involvement in development efforts has been observed in many African countries. Providing enough incentives for economic transformation has also become more challenging due to the state's weakened capacity to promote the equitable and efficient distribution of resources. The state must concentrate on three crucial responsibilities in order to bring about economic transformation in Africa: planning the development process, creating effective development policies, and putting those plans and policies into practice. The development process must be planned for some reason. Free-market forces, which frequently have communication and coordination issues, cannot make the best decisions since the necessary improvements are not marginal. Comprehensive development frameworks can address the interconnection of all development process components more effectively than limited partial models. Pervasive market failures characterise most economies in underdeveloped nations. The planning context is also ideal for considering information and coordination externalities associated with the development process. The state must surely develop effective development strategies and programs. However, the best way to do this task is to constantly discuss supply, demand, and consumption with important social and economic players. Maintaining macroeconomic stability is necessary to promote steady, fluctuation-free growth rates over the long run. Economic transformation necessitates the application of proper policies, incentives, and sanctions to ensure that public and private resources are directed in the direction where they will be used most efficiently. The construction of a developmental state to oversee the process may be necessary to achieve economic transformation for long-term, sustainable, and equitable growth in Africa in light of the abovementioned factors. The African state is "able to construct and deploy the institutional architecture within the state and mobilise society towards the realisation of its developmental project" when working "credibly, legitimately" in support of "industrialisation, economic growth, and the enhancement of human capabilities." There is no other way to express it. Still, highlighting those above, it is "a state that puts economic development as the top priority of government policy and can design effective instruments to promote such a goal". Using new chances for commerce and profitable manufacturing, weaving formal and informal networks of collaboration among citizens and authorities, and creating new formal institutions are a few of these tools. Having the political will and ability to develop and put into practice capacity-expanding, transformative, and distributive economic and social development policies that result from democratically-organised public deliberations and are unaffected by technocratic and socio-political elites defines an effective developmental state in Africa. This definition is based in large part on the capability-based development theory.

Among the key features of such a developmental state are the following:

1.   A government with the political will and legal authority to carry out the necessary tasks for a development vision held by the nation is a crucial factor.

2.   A key factor is good laws, upholding property rights, the rule of law, an impartial court, representative political institutions, a powerful central bank and other regulatory organisations.

3.   A competent, impartial administration guarantees that its strategies and programmes are implemented effectively and efficiently following recognised goals for national development.

4.   An interactive, institutionalised process whereby the political establishment and bureaucracy actively incorporate other societal actors (such as the private sector and civil society) in formulating, implementing, monitoring, and evaluating development programs.

5.   A comprehensive development framework that explicitly incorporates the complementarities between social and economic policies and establishing national development goals.

6.   A governance framework that guarantees that the complete spectrum of stakeholders and societal actors have thoroughly discussed and reached a consensus on the focus, context, contents and implementation modalities of the national development programme.

The developmental state approach could address development issues by restoring and enhancing state capacity to increase its ability to develop human potential and promote an equitable and efficient resource allocation. This should, in turn, create the right incentives for economic diversification and transformation. In an effort to achieve the intended socio-economic development outcome, the strategy should also prioritise establishing and bolstering financial and sociopolitical institutions and ensuring they work harmoniously. Additionally, it should enable the creation and implementation of macroeconomic, industrial, and sectoral policies that promote economic transformation and counteract any potentially negative effects of endowment, environment, and geography on the growth pattern of the continent. African countries must establish transformative institutions and democratic, ethical governments. Such organisations require strong leadership as a crucial component. In a developing country, the administration seeks to develop a plan of action that prioritises the populace's needs over personal interests.

Additionally, it should enable the creation and implementation of macroeconomic, industrial, and sectoral policies that promote economic transformation and counteract any potentially adverse effects of endowment, environment, and geography on the growth pattern of the continent. African countries must establish transformative institutions and democratic, ethical governments. Such organisations require strong leadership as a crucial component. In a developing nation, the government aims to create a strategy that puts the needs of the people ahead of individual interests. Leaders should take responsibility for a developmental program embodied in a vision to end underdevelopment. In order to achieve this, the leadership must be dedicated to industrialising Africa and creating more lucrative and productive job possibilities in the formal economy while being inclusive. The state must ensure that people can access sustainable work possibilities and opportunities to acquire assets essential to inclusivity. Land reform, for instance, will be crucial, especially in Southern Africa.

Additionally, in other subregions where subsistence agriculture is predominant, the state would be required to encourage cooperatives and provide small farmers access to markets, technology, business expertise and other resources. Some African nations may need to implement agrarian reform to develop into democratic states. The development of leadership skills is crucial at all levels. In this regard, the state must establish a capable and qualified bureaucracy and ensure that selection and advancement decisions are based on ability rather than political favouritism, ethnicity or religion. The formulation of national development goals in Africa must consider democratic public debates. The African state's participatory and consultative elements should enable civil society and social movement organisations to participate in development and governance. Institutionalising local and national deliberative procedures and processes is indeed necessary. African leaders should encourage citizen participation in national development initiatives. As a result, economic policy legitimacy and government transparency should both rise. The African Peer Review Mechanism, which some African nations have voluntarily adopted, has the potential to significantly contribute to the creation of such a democratic developmental state by systematising the involvement of other actors, particularly the private sector and civil society.

We will now consider economic growth. One of the numerous ways independent African states have continued to be subject to outside interference is through trade. Trade is one of the primary ways the African continent has been connected to the global economy since the end of colonial rule. The managers of the postcolonial state found themselves caught up in deeply ingrained commercial practices that they could scarcely escape because their economy was already set up to manufacture commodities to meet the industrial needs of wealthier nations (Nanji and Munchiri, 2009. p2). Africa's share of global commerce has decreased despite an increased trade orientation because its exports have expanded considerably more slowly than the rest. The UNCTAD Handbook of Statistics (2007) states that in 2004 Africa's exports comprised 1.6% of all exports globally. "In 2004, 1.4% of global imports came from Africa" (Alice Sindzingre, 2008. p9). According to those above, makes the region heavily dependent on export trade to maintain its balance of payments.

Since practically all of the states in that region produce the same types of items (primary products), they are not only forced to compete on the global stage for the same market partners, but the likelihood of a robust regional trade is also tiny (Nanji and Munchiri, 2009). Export-led growth is a development strategy that has been used with remarkable success in some regions of the world, particularly Asia, giving the impression that it could have been a lifeline for the majority of developing countries looking for a niche on the international economic scene (Theodore Cohn, 2008, p339). However, its implementation in other parts of the world, such as Africa, could result in real economic growth (Dani Rodrik, 2008). Export-led growth is a policy open to excessive volatility. Another policy would be Import Substitution Industrialization (ISI), which aimed to replace industrial imports with domestically manufactured goods (Cohn, p214). Most African nations embraced this policy to get a stronger foothold on the global market and develop their manufacturing capacities while lowering their reliance on Western countries for manufactured goods. The adoption of ISI policies hasn't been entirely successful, though.

Infant industries require much protection to compete in the global market. Maintaining democratic norms in the twenty-first century will require some work. Each nation must decide the type of democracy it wants based on experience. However, effective leadership and excellent governance must be implemented. Whatever the form of democracy, a few conditions must be met. If African development is to be successful, African nations must uphold economic and political rights. It should be recalled that the Asian Tigers developed and grew significantly while living under authoritarian governments. Democracy is, therefore, desirable but not necessary for economic liberation. However, for African countries to fulfil their progress and overcome their 21st-century challenges, economic governance must coexist with good governance (not democracy); concerns of transparency, accountability, a legal framework for conducting business etc., are essential components. Economic liberalisation is critical to restructuring the African economy and achieving economic growth. The pursuit of privatisation, openness and competition impacts Africa's economic development and expansion. The private sector is the growth engine, according to the underlying principle. However, the private sector must first grow in most African nations. The market's exuberance must be considered in light of its capacity to deliver the elements necessary to advance an economy on a macro level. The key is to allow the government to compete in the economy alongside interested economic players.

Avoiding both market and government failures will be the goal.

An economic structure represents the various sectors' relative output and factor utilisation contributions. As a result, as the economy expands, structural transformation can be seen as a change in the sectoral distribution of production and labour employment (that is, a real per capita GDP increases). African nations must maintain real per capita income growth over an extended period of time. Consider Malaysia, whose primary sector comprises natural resources (rubber and tin) and agriculture, which has typically been compared to many African nations in terms of initial circumstances, growing performance and development accomplishments. Unlike in many African nations, sharp social class, religion, and language divisions were prevalent.

Nevertheless, "the Malaysian growth story can be viewed as a narrative of the structural transformation of a largely agricultural economy to a more industrialised economy, and then to attempts to further transform it in the latter part of the 1990s towards a knowledge-based economy" (Yusof and Bhattasali, 2008: 30). The tale highlights, among other things, how important a state can be in transforming a struggling economy into a thriving one with a middle-class income in just three decades or fewer. The critical takeaway from Malaysia and other pertinent development experiences is that purposeful state intervention based on a systematic planning process to change the economy's structure was necessary for effective economic transformation. The data demonstrate that the state was involved in this process by drafting pertinent development policies, establishing essential institutions and allocating the required funding (Yusof and Bhattasali, 2008).

The examples of prosperous nations in Asia, Latin America and elsewhere present two crucial elements of efficient economic transformation processes; the first is that patterns of structural change, economic development methods in general, and industrialisation and diversification, in particular, have discernible common traits. The state is crucial to directing and fostering successful economic transformation, the second and most important feature. Solid and functional institutions are essential for successful transformation, as is developing infrastructure, luring foreign resources, and boosting productivity. However, many African nations have serious infrastructure problems, particularly concerning their energy infrastructure. Given the state's central role in economic transition, a "developmental state" strategy might be necessary. Evidence from numerous studies suggests that the profound structural economic transformation and sustained prosperity that occurred over a three-decade period in Japan, Korea, Malaysia, and Singapore were largely the result of a disciplined planning strategy. Most African countries could not experience long-term economic growth, so their economies did not significantly change structurally. As a result, the challenge of genuine development still exists. Governments must become more adept at selecting industries that match their endowment makeup and level of development. The government's policy to support industrial upgrading and diversification must be based on industries with a latent competitive advantage so that once the new sectors are created, they may quickly become competitive both locally and internationally. For African states to successfully restructure their economies, appropriate economic and social development plans and policies must be planned, created, and put into effect.

We'll now examine interdependence on a global scale. Globalisation is the process of integrating economic decision-making globally, including consumption, investment, and saving strategies. All nations are compelled to participate in this global market. Therefore, challenges must be ready and prepared for globalisation and the interdependence of states for them to develop and face the difficulties of the twenty-first century. According to Phillips (1999, p. 12), "countries which benefit most from globalisation are those which have met the basic needs of their people and in a sustained manner too". The structural makeup of African economies must change. In any case, globalisation is an additional strategy for giving industrialised nations access to larger markets. This concept may explain why wealthier countries welcomed NEPAD, and the Bretton Woods Institutions may help African nations take advantage of the advantages of globalisation. Underdeveloped nations' initiatives, the NEPAD framework and the private sector, should be encouraged to invest in African states, which would lessen factors such as inconsistent macroeconomic policies, policy reversals, insecurity, and uncertainty and increase investment in Africa.

There is evidence that excellent economic governance is needed to attract foreign investment. Thus, African governments must be prepared to provide specific guarantees if foreign investment is to be drawn. Globalisation is developing and expanding communication and interaction between nations and peoples. Technological advancements aid mobility, communication, political and military power, knowledge, skills and the blending of cultural and value systems and practices. Globalisation is not an innocent, value-free process that decides for itself. Others view it as the icing on the cake of successful socio-politico-economic, reciprocally beneficial global integration. While some see it as a risky exploitation process where wealthy governments and large international corporations are growing richer and richer at the expense of the poor, it is also seen as a sort of fulfilment of the adage "man to man is a wolf." Whatever one's perspective, the globalisation phenomenon has attracted enough attention to warrant extensive discussion at the United Nations General Assembly, which, in its resolution 55/102, acknowledged "globalisation and its impact on the full enjoyment of all human rights" and expressed the "need to achieve international cooperation in promoting and encouraging respect for human rights and fundamental freedoms for all without distinction" (relating to the right to dissent). It's crucial to remember that, optimistically, globalisation presents many advantages. However, it is perhaps more important to be honest about the drawbacks of globalisation, including the reality that its costs are unfairly dispersed across, within, and among nations, and its advantages are spread unequally. The above concept is remarkably accurate in the African countries' 1999 Human Development Report by the UNDP.

Suppose African countries want to thrive in the era of globalisation. In that case, they must implement the following policies: African states must build and strengthen change-oriented public administration systems to adapt to globalisation. They must also be open to risk, ambiguity and change, maintain transparency and responsibility toward the African populace, project an image of democracy and sensitivity to local issues, and take a proactive stance toward globalisation so that the difficulties and advantages can be anticipated and planned African nations ought to use globalisation to determine the course of their citizens. They should address the demand for human talent from all perspectives rather than letting globalisation operate their country and determine how the globe develops (skills, knowledge, attitude, networks and information technology).

In any event, globalisation or not, a nation can only be as developed as its people and resources allow. Address the lack of institutional ability (i.e., build or enhance adaptable institutions, global in their outlook and capable of meaningful interaction with other actors on the world stage). These institutions must be present across the board in politics and public administration, and they must be built with the ability to interact with other sectors of society and the business community. Adopt flexible administrative procedures rather than bureaucracy and rule enforcement that are self-serving and rigid. The context of African countries, particularly their needs and capacities, should always be considered when adopting "New Public Management techniques" (as they are known in industrialised nations). For instance, the shrinking of the state's borders, which included privatisation, retrenchment and reduction of public spending in social sectors like education and health, was probably not implemented in several African countries in the right amounts. Counteracting those, as mentioned earlier, African states should have their voices amplified in these international organisations so that the decisions made have the approval and input of the African leaders. Notably, this isn't true today in a lot of ways. Adopt and practice participatory governance engaging all actors, including the national, international, and local governments, the private sector and civil society. Invest in the health and education sectors to increase social capital. In other words, in light of globalisation, African nations should not seek to assign blame between rich and developing countries.

The African economy is still in its infancy after years of conceptualising, developing, and putting into action countless economic policies and programs. Africa is home to a rising proportion of the world's poorest people, but they are largely unable to influence how resources are allocated. Africa overtook Asia as the world's poorest continent when actual income was averaged. The majority of African countries continue to rely heavily on help, export primarily and are in debt. Regarding net present value, the foreign debt burden in 1997 was more significant than 80% of GDP. Africa is the only core region where investment and savings per capita have declined. The average African nation has the lowest savings rate in the world. Beyond low income, diminishing trade shares, poor savings, and slow growth, Africa faces several other development issues. If policies are not implemented, the continent will demonstrate excessive economic and development fragility and stay underdeveloped in the twenty-first century. Africa isn't developing because of insecurity, political uncertainty, and rivalry. Maintaining peace remains a top priority, and excellent governance and strong leadership are essential for post-conflict peacebuilding. The majority of African countries, however, have weak governance, poor management, and weak leadership.

Due to ineffective economic transformation, a lack of state of development adoption and other factors, economic growth is regarded as being very slow in many African countries. These factors prevent Africa from successfully addressing the challenges of the twenty-first century. The continent faces the adverse effects of the globalisation age, environmental degradation, food insecurity, pandemics, epidemics, the impact of regional integration and other market competitiveness issues with middle-income, developed-country rivals. One could argue that the write-up assesses the four main opportunities that Africa could use to overcome those difficulties, namely:

- Achieving peace, political stability, and security.

- Allowing nations to adopt good governance with solid leadership.

- Eradicating weak and ineffective government.

Economic transformation, one of the primary drivers of economic growth, is brought about by good governance and peace. With this, the continent should make the most of the constructive interconnection that has resulted from globalisation. If implemented by all stakeholders, the four integrative elements should guide and facilitate African development. The below sub-topics are other attitudes that can help build the African to contribute to positive change in Africa.

ARTIFICIAL INTELLIGENCE IN AFRICA

Artificial intelligence (AI) is being adopted and used more frequently worldwide. Economically, socially, and politically are just a few ways AI development and application are changing African lives and cultures. Because of the COVID-19 pandemic, these advances are already challenging to understand and forecast. It is essential to construct dynamic ecosystems based on the five stakeholders—policymakers, universities, large corporations, start-ups, and multi-stakeholder partnerships—who serve as the cornerstone of AI success to expand AI adoption in Africa. According to Li et al. (2018), Hamet and Tremblay (2017), and Adamopoulou and Moussiades (2020), artificial intelligence (AI) refers to a collection of technologies that enable robots to behave intelligently and emulate human sensing, comprehension, and action. Nearly all fields involving human intellect will be significantly impacted by technology. Businesses and institutions can use it to enhance operations, stimulate innovations, empower workers, and personalise activities. AI alters human behaviour, enabling more effective resource management, boosting productivity and improving public service delivery. Remarkably, the use of AI in governance, health care, agriculture, commerce, and education is significantly impacting these fields. Artificial intelligence (AI), a specialised area quickly expanding, could alter every aspect of human social interactions. Around the world, AI-powered services are present in many facets of daily life, yet adoption rates differ between developed and developing countries. The penetration of AI into the African social system through diverse operations is evident (Schoeman et al. 2021; Marino Garcia and Kelly 2020).

For instance, chatbots in Kenya can now treat patients without them having to go to the doctor, and a data-driven platform called Zenvus in Nigeria gives farmers insights. Finance and other industries are not exempt either; AI-powered technologies are altering how these industries operate. Mobile Money and Mukuru in South Africa make transferring money between other African nations simple and quick. Kudi is an AI-powered chatbot from Nigeria that promises to offer financial services to those who are less fortunate. TakeAlot and Konga are two further online retailers in Africa. There is anticipation that AI technologies will be the next wave of technologies to acquire general acceptance because of the increasing use of mobile devices in Africa. However, the widespread adoption of AI applications in Africa has not yet happened, except for a few countries (such as South Africa, Nigeria, Ethiopia, Kenya, and Ghana) (Gadzala 2018). Most of Africa tragically lacks the essential elements required for technology adoption, and many African nations still lack the infrastructure, governance, data ecology, STEM education, and other components needed for AI.

This chapter examines the obstacles to the general adoption of AI throughout Africa. Therefore, the inquiry is: "What are the challenges facing the design, development, deployment, and application of AI in Africa?" A desk study was conducted to review the literature (including reports) on AI in Africa. The industrialised nations of the globe are now developing, deploying, and applying AI technology significantly more than in Africa. These happenings in the above-said countries are due to contextual considerations, which may be considered barriers that must be addressed to enhance AI capabilities. This chapter identifies these obstacles and hurdles and offers suggestions to help create, introduce, and apply AI technology in Africa.

While some African countries, including Mauritius, Egypt, Zambia, Tunisia, and Botswana, have acknowledged the potential of AI to increase GDP and have developed national AI strategies, all are still in the early stages. This is even though South Africa, Nigeria, and Kenya have passed data protection laws. The African Union (AU) recommends establishing structured regulation of AI laws and regulations to limit the benefits of technology for Africans. Most Africans adopt technology slowly and with a "wait and see" attitude, making them laggard innovators and late majority adopters. The AU must move quickly to build a well-structured adoption and implementation strategy to increase the acceptance of AI-powered technologies throughout the African populace. Overall, there is a shortage of pertinent policies that may prioritise the development and application of AI while addressing potential social repercussions. In the context of technology development, ethics refers to guidelines for the best conduct that can be observed and followed during developing and applying novel and developing technologies. These guidelines are based on cultural norms, religious beliefs, and public acceptance. Ethics are the cornerstone of human endeavours in Africa that can support African cultures and foster confidence in advancing and using technologies there. While AI has great potential, it also presents significant challenges for governments and enterprises, particularly regarding ethics. Many African nations still debate the Second and Third Industrial Revolutions' ethical, financial, and social effects. AI has already been linked to several ethical problems. Studies have identified several significant areas of AI's potential effects on African society, such as accountability, data bias, transparency, and socio-economic hazards. "AI technologies are systems that mimic human intelligence. AI undermines established moral and legal paradigms that place human agency solely in the hands of humans. Using biased data, AI has been noted to create socio-economic inequality" (Larsson et al. 2019Additionally, creating AI systems requires sophisticated algorithms, which undermine transparency and trust. In the interest of training these algorithms, data is used. Many algorithms may not be properly tailored to the characteristics of local communities, according to claims that there is a data shortage in Africa and that the majority of data obtained does not accurately reflect the African experience. Stakeholders must engage in open talks about the ethical implications of AI and take required action in order to establish a solid foundation for AI adoption in Africa. Adopting AI technologies in Africa has additional difficulties due to user attitudes. Adopters' perspectives on accepting and rejecting an invention can be positive, negative, or uneasy." attitudes are a primary predictive factor impacting the adoption of a new product; hence, a better knowledge of attitudes in a well-defined manner is required" (Wang et al. 2008). Due to cultural and social influences, Africans are sceptical about adopting and using new technology. In a study on adopting AI in higher education, Chatterjee and Bhattacharjee (2020) revealed that "attitudes influence individuals' behavioural intentions to use AI". Likewise, another research on adopting software engineering products proved that user attitude influences the adoption of software tools (Okonkwo et al., 2019). The information above leads to the conclusion that higher education authorities would find it beneficial to mould stakeholders' attitudes to shape their intentions and behaviour. As a result, if students have negative perceptions of Chatbot technology applications in education, they will be hesitant to adopt and use the technology. Positive perception of innovation accelerates adoption. Inadequate infrastructure and network affordability are major hurdles to AI adoption in Africa. The growth of infrastructural development and mobile technology network connectivity in Africa is slow. A good percentage of Africa's population is unconnected and lacks internet access. The adoption of AI requires adequate availability of wireless network connectivity. In addition, African countries have the world's most expensive broadband. "The Alliance for Affordable Internet (A4AI) reported that African countries inhabited nine of the ten least affordable spots for internet access, with expenditures ranging from 12 to 44% of GDP" (Marino Garcia and Kelly 2020). Adopting and using any innovation, including AI, require the necessary competence. First and foremost, AI skill is much more difficult to perfect, and there is a greater demand for AI expertise. In order to inspire people to be interested in utilising AI to carry out their duties, it is crucial to provide favourable environments in the commercial, health, educational, and public ecosystems. They will gain these abilities thanks to this inspiration. The educational curriculum needs to be improved in order to incorporate the teaching of AI skills starting at the secondary level. People can learn AI skills by developing their mathematical and computer coding aptitudes. Since AI systems are present in every part of society, everyone should be familiar with them. All fields of study could benefit from adding beginning programming and computer science courses to help students learn AI-related skills. All stakeholders (citizens, policymakers, and technical experts) should be involved early in the architectural design process so that societal expectations, fears and concerns are considered, and no patchwork is necessary later as an afterthought. This course will improve users' knowledge of the system, reducing uncertainty or fear of the unknown. A responsible data management framework considering data diversity is recommended for AI developers. The framework will make it easier to collect comprehensive data for system development and improve the accuracy of AI system operations. Ethical challenges are big concerns regarding the adoption of AI systems in Africa. Many initiatives, including educational institutions, government agencies, non-governmental groups, and industry, have attempted to address AI technology's ethical and legal challenges. "However, the impact of these efforts is still insignificant in Africa" (Borenstein and Howard 2021). AI technology's selection, design, deployment, and usage have ethical implications.

Therefore, we concur with Borenstein and Howard's (2021) recommendations that developers acknowledge the ethical dimensions that are intertwined with the technology they are producing and that it is their essential responsibility to do so. Increasing developer awareness of their moral obligations and professional responsibilities will help to reduce ethical problems. In order to direct the growth of AI, the government and other professional groups should tighten their ethics policies. Making a favourable environment stimulates creative thinking—still having difficulty developing its infrastructure in Africa. Most government programs prioritise urban growth at the expense of rural areas. Government should make sure that projects are expanded to rural areas, giving reliable and sufficient network coverage to all communities. For instance, most rural farming businesses use AI to improve operations and maximise output. Additionally, to lay the groundwork for creating and applying AI technologies, the African Union and each African country should establish AI strategies and policies.

Last but not least, the economies of Africa are still under development and need technology to grow faster. As a result, the continent must support the use of AI in numerous contexts and for a variety of purposes. As part of a public awareness campaign, it should be encouraged to establish various organisations that can help address citizens' concerns and anxieties. These organisations ought to encourage the use of AI in Africa and develop effective methods for resolving its social consequences. The government and business sector should promote the establishment of technology start-ups or tech centres to educate the upcoming generation of AI specialists.

Adopting AI technology in Africa is difficult due to a lack of technical expertise, uncertainties, structured data, government regulations, moral concerns, and user attitudes. A company may use AI to increase productivity while remaining competitive and learning more in-depth customer information. However, there aren't enough people with the knowledge and skills to run these programs. A strong skill set is needed to develop an AI technology with good content, system, and service qualities. To use the technology efficiently, one needs to have sufficient product expertise. These abilities go beyond rudimentary technological understanding and may address other issues like a lack of administrative expertise or coming up with commercial concepts. Artificial intelligence (AI) tools need routine upkeep and upgrades, necessitating skilled programming skills. In other words, a business that wishes to adopt AI technologies needs an inside engineer or a dependable vendor for upkeep and services.

Business executives, other interested parties, and members of the public who may be involved in implementing and using any AI must therefore have the fundamental abilities necessary to adapt, understand, and use the technology in their particular fields of endeavour. In other words, from the early years of elementary education through the professional level, all parties involved, including the government, should devise ways to help people acquire the necessary skills. A lack of technical expertise hampers the adoption and application of technologies. Applying AI technologies presents ethical questions regarding personality, culture, transparency, and privacy. The use of AI raises a number of ethical issues, including the following: Are AIs destroying jobs? How are data used and stored? Is AI more intelligent than people? ... and so on. These queries raise doubts and fears about the use of AI technologies.

AI, for instance, gathers patient data in many formats throughout the healthcare system. Many privacy issues are raised by collecting user data; some may have legal support and are covered by data-protection legislation (Ruane et al., 2019). User privacy must be taken into account whenever AI is used in any element of life. It is best to let people know that a system is an artificial intelligence machine so they may choose how to interact with it intelligently. Human-to-human interactions are different from those with machines. The user's understanding and trust will grow as they become more aware of an AI system's nature. While designing and developing AI technologies, user groups, interests, characteristics, and circumstances should be taken into account to accommodate various users.

"Culture plays an essential role in ethics. It is concerned with the social behaviour of people in a specific area. African nations are multilingual and have diverse cultural backgrounds, which can impact the adoption of technological innovation. According to research conducted in Nigeria and South Africa, culture determines technological innovation" (Bankole et al. 2011; Lekhanya 2013). When creating AI systems, individual beliefs and sentiments should be taken into account. An innovative technology's adoption is influenced by how its users perceive it. Users are more likely to accept and employ AI technologies when their perceptions are good, as opposed to when they are negative. Users will be sceptical of innovation's use if they lack sufficient information, which will cause uncertainty—fear of the unknown. Because most Africans are laggards and late majority adopters, they are uncertain of new technological innovations and employ a wait-and-see approach to adopting innovations. The greater the level of uncertainty, the lower the adoption of AI in Africa. Developers and other stakeholders should always strive to make AI systems user-friendly to reduce the tension of new technology. Governments should step up infrastructural development and expansion of network connectivity, especially in rural locations in Africa.

In order to ensure proper AI system development, deployment, and adoption in Africa, African governments and stakeholders, including the African mobile ecosystem, must set up well-structured rules and policies. AI is a rapidly developing field employed in various fields, such as business, politics, education, and social activities. Adopting AI technologies may help attain the sustainable development that Africa still needs. Using AI technologies as supporting tools will be impossible if they are not properly adopted. In order for AI to become widely adopted, these issues must be solved.

A. I. technologies have a huge potential to support human flourishing and the expansion of African economies. AI technology can change how businesses operate and perform, increase productivity, and improve Africa's access to transportation, health care, and education. Africa will continue to lag behind other nations in the international community if these difficulties or obstacles are not addressed. African stakeholders, particularly politicians, must establish strong governance infrastructures and processes to advance AI design, development, adoption, and application. Along with policymakers, industry players must concentrate on capacity building to guarantee that sufficient AI skills are obtained for the ethical use of AI to solve the requirements and problems unique to Africa. Therefore, it is intended that thorough comprehension and awareness of these difficulties and suggestions will be attained to ensure expedited AI design, development, and acceptance, which will substantially impact the continent's economy.

The potential for AI to improve health is immense. Improved diagnosis surveillance, epidemic response, and management of health systems are some of these potentials, particularly in low- and middle-income nations. In India, Kenya, Malawi, South Africa, Rwanda, and Zambia, a cervical cancer screening tool based on AI has previously undergone testing.AI may also help diagnose diseases like Covid-19 and TB early.

African countries should create policies at the local level to dispel the various misconceptions about AI. In Nairobi,

Kenya, more than a thousand young people have received training in AI algorithms. By the end of this decade, around eleven million young people are anticipated to enter the labour force yearly. Fears are understandable, especially in light of the technological revolution that artificial intelligence (AI) is causing. Not knowing AI and its workings causes a lot of concern. Africa should promote and establish forums on AI deep learning. However, only those in the tech industry should have access to this topic.AI is a vast field of computer science. There have to be laws that educate Africans about artificial intelligence.

AI stands out as the enticing instrument to build a prosperous, secure, and safe Africa.

The original research thoroughly examines the major variables and communities influencing the ecosystem across the continent through statistics and trends. Africa is at a critical crossroads right now, and by adopting AI, the continent has much potential for a better future. In the age of artificial intelligence and smart technology, "I am aware of the opportunity this new Africa represents." John Kamara, a co-founder of Aice & Afyarekod, wrote the report's foreword, which covered the opportunities that abound with the usage of data and solutions that can have an influence on people's lives in the areas of health, education, deep technology, research, fintech, agri-tech, and climate impact. Because of this, Kamara exhorts Africa to "embrace and adopt AI as a key, if not the most important, form of technology to ensure we are truly part of the 4th Industrial Revolution."

CHAPTER 6

MEASURES AND STRUCTURES TO SUPPORT CREATIVITY AND TALENTS IN AFRICA

When analysing the relative development of human resources over the past 40 years, it is impossible to ignore that Africa has lagged far behind the rest of the globe. The "brain drain" issue has harmed Africa more than any other region. The issue is now of special concern due to the severe scarcity of qualified academics and researchers that African institutions of higher learning and research are currently suffering. Since Africa is losing its capacity to innovate and undertake the research necessary to contribute to the growth and application of global knowledge—knowledge needed to discover solutions to the most pressing problems of our time—the situation is growing worse. Critical global issues like eradicating hunger and extreme poverty, disease, violent conflict, security concerns, migration, environmental degradation, etc., demand quick study. Given this urgency, it is not advisable to disregard or think that Africa has no impact,

Many African countries are currently dealing with a severe issue—a shortage of competent workers- that they cannot resolve in the near or medium term. Additionally, Africa needs a tremendous capacity infusion across all industries and levels. For instance, due to a lack of qualified workers in many African nations, public and commercial sectors are underperforming and failing to give the people the services they need. In order to partially ameliorate the shortage of qualified persons in Africa shortly and slightly longer term, it is crucial to mobilise the intellectual capital of the African diaspora living in the West for "brain circulation" aims. This course allows the highly skilled African diaspora to play a leading and proactive role in "brain gain" aimed at Africa. Designing policies to utilise the massive untapped human capital of the African diaspora in the Netherlands and other parts of Europe for Africa's benefit is urgently needed. In order to better utilise the vast intellectual capital and the "brain reserve" of the African diaspora for the advancement of knowledge in Africa, it may be more effective to strategically mainstream their intellectual capital into the overall development policy proposals of the Netherlands that are being developed to address the brain drain problem in Africa. The qualified African diaspora's skills profile reveals their strong science and technology abilities. For instance, 7 out of the 30 respondents had doctorates in engineering, environmental, natural, or agricultural sciences, all of which are very pertinent to Africa. According to their profiles, they obtained their broad teaching and research backgrounds through attachments—some of which lasted longer than ten years—to universities and research organisations in the Netherlands. In addition, 2 of the 30 people interviewed are doctors, 6 are PhD candidates in science and technology, 1 has a master's degree in engineering, and another has a bachelor's degree in information technology. 4 of the 30 questioned respondents also have master's degrees in economics. This outcome is because a substantial section of the selected African diaspora has scientific and technological know-how highly valued by African schools.

6 out of the 30 participants interviewed hold doctorates in linguistics, political science, economics, educational policy, or a combination of these fields. Additionally, they have broad experiences in both teaching and research from Dutch universities and research centres. In addition, 3 of the 30 respondents had master's degrees in media

communication and development sociology. The study of the 30 highly talented people of the African diaspora's skill profiles shows a vast knowledge, teaching, and research capacity that may be used to improve knowledge development in African universities. Some of the highly educated African diasporans who were interviewed admitted that their skills are either not used because they are unemployed or underused since they are working in positions in the Netherlands that are well below their qualifications. "The under-utilised and the unutilised knowledge capital of the African diaspora in the Netherlands should be made available to Africa where it is badly needed through appropriately designed schemes and programs before becoming wasted," one interviewee suggested. Some interviewees are concerned that if their skills are not used, they will eventually lose them and be unable to support progress in both the host nation and their own country when they return.

According to some highly skilled African diaspora members surveyed, Africa falls short in science and technology. If properly utilised and deployed, these scientific skills can enhance Africa; they are crucial to encourage and speed economic growth and development. More importantly, advanced technology and skills enable countries to address local issues related to agricultural production, water supply, health, and other sectors. However, because of a lack of scientific understanding, Africa is unable to end its current state of poverty. Several respondents put out two explanations to explain Africa's poor scientific development. The first is that the majority of skilled workers have left Africa, mostly because those with degrees in science, engineering, medicine, or accounting were in high demand and appreciated elsewhere. The second cause is the poor enrollment in science and technical subjects at African universities. Due to a lack of facilities and equipment, as well as a migration of lecturers, teachers, and instructors with the necessary training, African institutions are unable to enrol more students in the sciences. Africa has already been marginalised in terms of the advancement of scientific knowledge globally due to its low levels of scientific proficiency. According to the Commission for Africa's most recent report, "Our Common Interest," the issue is serious. "Skilled professionals are key to building improvements in the administration and technical ability which Africa so gravely lacks," the report stated. The report then makes the following suggestion: "The international community should have committed in 2005 US$500 million per year, over ten years, to revitalise Africa's higher education institutions and up to US$3 billion over ten years to develop centres of excellence in science and technology, including African institutes of technology."

In general, the 30 highly skilled members of the African diaspora who were surveyed expressed a readiness to volunteer their time to advance knowledge in Africa. Only one who is now jobless made the ability to secure employment and sustain herself a requirement for her readiness to voluntarily contribute to advancing African knowledge. Additionally, these people are prepared and available to provide free summer courses, plan seminars and workshops, evaluate teaching and training curricula, etc. In response, they all said they would provide free coaching and lectures as part of their voluntary effort to spread knowledge throughout Africa. As one interviewee succinctly put it, this is a means of giving something back to the culture from which we came. They merely demanded that their lodging, travel, and daily living costs while on assignment be paid for. One interviewee cited the argument that "a personal financial burden can reduce the interest of any volunteer and can even discourage a committed and proactive volunteer" as support for their position. Some interviewees said they were ready to attend any university in any African nation where their knowledge and experience would be most respected and required. They believe it is not necessary to aid their own countries merely and that assisting any country or region in Africa with an enabling environment is feasible. In order to facilitate and effectively coordinate the partnership efforts between the diasporan professionals in the Netherlands and institutes of higher learning in Africa, the interviewees highlighted the need to establish a diaspora organisation. Thus, the 30 suitable African diasporans who were questioned showed a clear interest, a commitment, and a strong desire to share knowledge and contribute to advancing skills in Africa. More importantly, if given the chance, as some of them put it, to impart their knowledge and professional experiences to others back home, they are willing to perform this work voluntarily. During the data collection for this study, we noticed that the highly educated African diasporans living in the Netherlands are becoming increasingly aware of their obligation to help the continent they physically left behind but have not emotionally abandoned. Some interviewees offered a cost-free method of knowledge transfer to African universities. They specifically mentioned that it would be cost-free if summer courses were scheduled to coincide with the personal visits of knowledgeable diaspora residents eager to contribute to knowledge development projects while back home. In such situations, there would be no need to pay travel charges or other associated costs since the person would already be travelling home for a holiday. However, sufficient preparation and cooperation would be necessary. According to one interviewee, it would necessitate the existence (or establishment) of a network (or networks) in the host country that complies with a skills database of the diaspora experts along subject lines and makes that database accessible to the various departments and faculties at the universities in the homeland. Once in email communication, the departments would regularly update the talented academics or scholars from the native diaspora about the conferences, lectures, and workshops scheduled for the coming year. Once a formal relationship has been established, diaspora scholars will be able to notify departments that focus on their areas of expertise in advance of their intended arrival and indicate their willingness to give lectures, brief training sessions, workshops, seminars, and other types of presentations when they decide to travel back to their home countries. Departures from colleges in the homelands, diaspora networks and organisations in the host countries, and in certain cases, the embassies of the African diaspora homelands in the host countries would all need to participate in and collaborate on such an initiative actively. It would be wise to take advantage of the highly qualified African diaspora's willingness to transfer their expertise to African colleges freely and offer their services without charge. Nevertheless, despite its appeal, this kind of interaction is still ad hoc, intermittent, and restricted in scope when addressing Africa's serious brain drain issue. In light of this, some respondents recommended that a more ongoing and planned approach to solving the problem is needed in addition to this sporadic interaction. Given those mentioned above, it is clear that African universities and other knowledge institutions require a significant increase in capacity. Sporadic and insufficient attempts cannot satisfactorily and effectively meet this requirement. Therefore, a brief practical proposal for harnessing the abilities of those in the diaspora to transfer knowledge to Africa systematically is presented below. An effective policy idea that merits consideration proposes that academics from the African diaspora might systematically transfer knowledge by working in African colleges for three months a year. For instance, a scholar from the African diaspora is willing to work three months each year for free at a university in Africa while continuing to be employed by the Dutch university or other academic organisation they are affiliated with. This means that the university that hired the African Diaspora Scholar in the Netherlands would be responsible for paying their salary for the three months they spent there. The transfer of information through academics in the African diaspora could raise the educational standards at African universities through this continuous and organised involvement. Therefore, given that it is likely to produce more benefit than sporadic and irregular efforts, it is crucial to actively investigate the prospect of building such a structured approach to transferring knowledge to Africa. The African diaspora working in other institutions and sectors in the Netherlands who may be able to transfer knowledge to Africa, assist in building or improving networks, and bring their experience to Africa are also covered by this structured approach to knowledge transfer. For instance, a hospital doctor might work three months a year in an African hospital while still receiving pay from the Dutch hospital he is affiliated with. Given that numerous and varied Dutch institutions and the public and commercial sectors may be more widely mobilised to support skills development in Africa, this scenario is arguably the most suited. The need for capacity building and skill development in African public and private institutions is enormous. They can only be addressed by broad, persistent participation over an extended length of time. Therefore, in order to complete this enormous work, it will be necessary to mobilise not just the professional African diaspora but also the institutions in the Netherlands and other Western nations with which they are affiliated. Because the host nations are endowed with significant human capital, equipment, and resources that may be used for the development of Africa, their involvement in the process is of the utmost importance. Furthermore, the efforts made to advance development in Africa will be made easier by the institutions that the African diaspora works with actively in the host nation to set up part-time placement in a particular African sector.

The highly competent African diasporans who were interviewed acknowledged several obstacles they had to overcome to bring knowledge back to their home countries and all of Africa. Additionally, these issues continue to exist and obstruct the transfer of their intellectual capital to the continent. The issues mentioned, and the difficulties described varied from university to university and from one country to another. Whatever the causes of these issues and limitations, the overall impact has been disastrous for the growth of the continent's knowledge institutions in many African nations. Civil conflicts, poor governance, political instability, and deplorable economic conditions are just a few of the country-level issues that, according to the respondents, prompted them to leave their home countries in the first place and continue to restrict or hinder the transfer of knowledge to Africa. These difficult problems—often referred to as "push factors"—have to do with the circumstances in the exporting countries that force the educated class to migrate overseas. They primarily show up as widespread social unrest, interruptions in economic activity, slow growth, high unemployment rates, depressed working conditions, poor physical infrastructure, inadequate social services, a lack of democracy, and human rights violations. The main issue that has forced some African diasporans interviewed to flee their countries and look for safety elsewhere is conflict and civil war. Some people who were interviewed claimed they left their homes to flee raging civil wars and ongoing conflicts in places like Mozambique, Somalia, Sudan, etc. In addition, protracted internal conflicts have damaged the resilience of social organisations, particularly academic institutions, in those nations by destroying their basic physical infrastructures. Even while some of the protracted civil wars are now gone, their negative consequences have left terrible repercussions that will take a long time to undo. As a result, there are poor living circumstances and no environment that would help draw in highly qualified diaspora scholars from other countries. This finding explains why several interviewees claimed that even if they now experience less personal uncertainty in their home countries than they did previously, the circumstance nevertheless acts as a deterrent to them making a sacrifice in their careers and permanently relocating there. The interviewees from the diaspora also mentioned that the prevalence of nepotism and the significance of political ties were factors in their decision to leave their own countries; they assert that these conditions are still present in much of the continent. The shortage and declining supply of economic resources mostly cause these issues. Thus, competition for scarce employment leads to political and personal connections taking precedence over expertise and talent. According to one interviewee, the issue in Africa is less a dearth of highly talented workers as it is a lack of economic capacity to take in educated individuals and provide them with incentives to stay on the continent. In many African nations, he noted, the lack of economic capacity leads to underfunded and under-resourced institutions of higher learning, making them too unattractive to draw in new academic staff, let alone keep those who are already working overseas. This interviewee went on to say that strengthening the economy has to be the first requirement for addressing the brain drain issue in Africa. However, it should be underlined that while economic expansion is essential, development itself cannot occur when, as in many African nations today, a large portion of the trained labour force is outside. For instance, according to a study by the International Organization for Migration, 30% of Africa's highly qualified labour force is already working overseas, providing a stark picture of the continent's severe human resource shortage. As a result, many African nations are faced with a painful conundrum: without economic growth, skilled workers cannot be kept, and without them, economic expansion is impossible. Simply put, many African nations are trapped in a vicious cycle that prevents them from experiencing the potential economic growth they could. The state of affairs in Africa is worrying in this regard. Given the restricted supply of its human capital, Africa is more vulnerable than other emerging nations because even a small loss of talented and educated workers can undermine growth and well-being. For instance, the World Markets Research Centre stated that "Africa's ongoing development efforts will continue to be undermined as long as the current phenomenon of human capital flight, or "brain drain," as it is commonly known, continues. Despite the numerous complex problems mentioned above, Africa has seen positive developments. Some of the interviewees from the diaspora brought up the previously discussed issue. They claim that efforts are being made to establish an environment encouraging Africans in the diaspora to participate in the continent's general development. To strengthen the intellectual capital, transnational networks, financial resources, and commercial savvy of the African countries, for instance, policies are being developed at both the national and continental levels to reconnect the African diaspora with their homelands. These policies have been implemented in response to the dramatic rise in skilled labour migration and the severe human resource shortages many African nations are currently experiencing. The brain drain stunts economic growth and depletes the continent's human resources. According to World Bank research, approximately 70,000 highly skilled African professionals, specialists, scholars, and managers with internationally marketable abilities migrate to industrialised nations for better job possibilities each year. As a result, in order to solve the issue, some African nations, including Ghana and Eritrea, have implemented policy adjustments that give these emigrants dual nationality and the ability to vote in their home nations. One African nation, Ghana, particularly, has a third of its highly educated and skilled labour force living overseas. Similarly, Olusegun Obasanjo, the former president of Nigeria, created a special advisor for the diaspora during his administration. The governments of Mali and Senegal have also established Ministries of Foreign and Diaspora Affairs, which are specifically responsible for overseeing and facilitating connections with citizens of those countries who reside overseas. In addition, several other African nations, including Liberia, Rwanda, and Sierra Leone, have previously conducted several conferences on the diaspora to examine and investigate ways the diaspora might actively contribute to development in the homelands. The African Union (AU) and NEPAD are currently courting the African diaspora on a continental basis. Focusing on the aforementioned indicates that Africa adapts to changing circumstances and desires to take advantage of the resources within its sizable expatriate community abroad. For instance, one of the AU's strategic objectives is to actively involve the diaspora in advancing democracy and development in Africa. By doing this, the AU aims to build a partnership for the benefit of Africa and acknowledge the diaspora as a force for good change on the continent. The African Union wants to work with the diaspora to create a better Africa that would make them proud of their heritage, said Amara Essy-Interim, Chairman of the AU, while addressing an African diaspora conference in Washington, DC. The fundamental idea is to seek a partnership different from the previous one. The AU is not merely concerned with monetary support from the diaspora. We simply want to put your intellectual power at the African Union's disposal. Thus, it is not anticipated that our collaboration will be a one-way process in which we merely take from the diaspora and do not provide anything in return. Africans on the continent and those living abroad must work together to help one another. Given how crucial the diaspora is to the African Union, some of its members have even urged that one of the commissioners be a person from the diaspora.

The diaspora will therefore be the sixth region of the African Union (West Africa, 20- 26 January 2003:25). This high-level solicitous approach indicates the value and premium placed on the economic, intellectual capital and transnational networking links that the African diaspora possess, and which need to be effectively harnessed for development in Africa. Similarly, the New Partnership for Africa's Development (NEPAD), attempting to reach out to the diaspora, also calls for establishing a reliable and continental database on the brain drain to determine the magnitude of the problem and promote collaboration between the diaspora and those on the continent. An important NEPAD priority of particular interest to this project is the proposal to develop the human resources capacity of Africa and reverse the brain drain. Furthermore, under NEPAD, African leaders explicitly call for creating the "necessary political, social and economic conditions that would serve as incentives to curb the brain drain". Thus Africa, at both the country and continental levels, is addressing vexing policy issues that have previously frustrated the diaspora and made it impossible for the African diaspora to contribute to economic and intellectual development on the continent. The policy change is creating an enabling environment badly needed to entice the diaspora in several countries on the continent.

Several interviewees feel that in-depth discussions and deliberations with these institutions' representatives are necessary to determine the practical procedures and potential scenarios of collaborations with the AAU and NEPAD. These difficulties, however, are outside the purview of this preliminary survey, which is only the first stage of the study. These concerns will be covered in greater detail in the study's second phase through additional research and fieldwork at African universities. However, some of the African diasporas suggested that Nuffic immediately organise a follow-up expert meeting with the 30 highly qualified African diasporas who were interviewed for this feasibility study, as well as representatives of the AAU, NEPAD, and perhaps other less significant associations of universities like SARUA, in order to capitalise on the momentum. The purpose of this discussion is to discuss the outcomes of this study and to share opinions, viewpoints, experiences, positive examples from the past, best practices, and practical approaches that can be used to put this diaspora-focused brain gain program into action. Another goal would be to generate draft legislative ideas that could make it easier for members of the highly educated African diaspora in the Netherlands and representatives of the AAU and NEPAD institutions to collaborate and partner on projects related to knowledge development in Africa.

MEASURES AFRICA CAN PUT IN PLACE TO PROMOTE TOURISM FOR INCREASED REVENUE

The tourism sector contributes significantly to GDP, employment, and trade in many African economies, and it is expanding mostly as a result of travellers from the continent itself. Most African nations still encounter significant challenges and constraints in their efforts to fully utilise the potential of tourism services for trade and economic growth. The Economic Development in Africa Report 2017 examines tourism's potential role in inclusive and transformative growth. The continent's tourist sector is growing when Africa boosts its production capacity, fosters regional integration, and pursues economic diversification. Africa should implement policies that build intersectoral ties, encourage intraregional travel, and advance peace to utilise better the tourist sector's capacity to assist equitable growth, structural transformation, and achieving the Sustainable Development Goals. The UN declared 2017 The International Year of Sustainable Tourism for Development. The tourist sector has been praised for its capacity to promote economic growth by fostering entrepreneurship, attracting investment, and job creation. If used effectively, it can also support the protection of cultural heritage, the advancement of community empowerment, and the preservation of ecosystems and biodiversity. Tourism can support both inclusive economic growth and sustainable growth. Since the 1990s, tourism has played a major role in Africa's growth, employment, and trade. Between 1995 and 2014, there was an average 6% increase in foreign tourists visiting Africa, while tourism export revenues climbed by 9% yearly. Between 2011 and 2014, or from 6.8% to 8.5% of the GDP in Africa, the average annual contribution of tourism to the world's gross domestic product (GDP) climbed from $69 billion to $166 billion between 1995 and 1998. Additionally, the average number of jobs created by tourism between 2011 and 2014 was above 21 million, or 7.1% of all jobs in Africa. According to the analysis above, the tourism industry supported one out of every fourteen employment between 2011 and 2014. Additionally connected to tourism are its independent operation from other economic sectors, major money leakage, escalation of sociocultural disputes, and environmental impact. History demonstrates that countries cannot only rely on tourism to lift their citizens out of poverty or spur long-term economic progress. The potential of tourism has been acknowledged by policymakers at the national and international levels, and national and international policy frameworks increasingly reflect this. SDGs 8, 12, and 14 emphasise the significance of tourism for local cultural promotion, economic growth, and job creation. However, because it affects many different sectors and is a cross-cutting issue, the rise of tourism impacts a number of Sustainable Development Goals, including infrastructure development, a decent job, gender equality, and poverty. In order to promote inclusion by including women and young people in the sector's activities and to spur growth in other productive sectors, the African Union's Agenda 2063 and the Tourism Action Plan under its New Partnership for Africa's Development both acknowledge the significance of tourism in driving socio-economic development and structural transformation in Africa. The 1998 Protocol on Tourism of the South African Development Community, the Sustainable Tourism Development Framework of the Common Market for Eastern and Southern Africa, and the Sustainable Tourism Master Plan 2013–2023 of the Intergovernmental Authority on Development all highlight the role that tourism plays in fostering socio-economic development at the regional level. Most African nations have national development plans that outline their future vision and specify planned policies and sectoral objectives, with the importance of tourism being highlighted. Tourism for Transformative and Inclusive Growth, The Economic Development in Africa Report

2017 investigates the contribution of tourism to African development. It contends that tourism can be a catalyst for inclusive growth and economic development in the correct policy environment and works in tandem with other initiatives to promote economic diversification and structural change. Since these topics have been covered in considerably more length in recent publications on the industry, the paper does not concentrate on climate change or its funding implications. The emphasis is on boosting tourism's contribution to economic growth, reducing poverty, trade, fostering regional integration, and structural change. To do this, Africa must overcome the main obstacle impeding the expansion of the travel and tourism sector—a lack of intersectoral linkages. For several reasons, tourism may be a significant contribution to economic growth. Specifically: Tourism greatly impacts the economy, jobs, and export revenue. The industry can make a strong case for prioritising African socio-economic development. The tourism industry has a relatively high employment rate for women and young people. Half of the workforce in the tourist industry is under the age of 25, and between 60 and 70 per cent of its workers are women globally. Thus, it could encourage more inclusive growth. The outlook for tourism is favourable due to increased disposable incomes, which result in more resources being accessible for leisure and travel, as well as globalisation, which encourages corporate travel. "International tourist arrivals to Africa are expected to reach 134 million by 2030" (World Tourism Organization, 2016). There is more room for promoting intraregional and continental travel in Africa, given that most foreign travel occurs inside a traveller's region internationally and that continental disposable incomes are anticipated to increase with a developing African middle class.

Tourism can also increase and disperse incomes through greater connections, which has significant knock-on consequences for reducing poverty. Strong connections stimulate a multiplier effect that can lead to widespread economic gains at the national level, local employment prospects and poverty alleviation. Tourism connections, however, are still insufficient and underutilised in many African nations. Therefore, a large portion of the value generated by the tourist sector is captured by foreign investors, international tour operators, and foreign airline corporations. At the same time, only modest advantages frequently reach those impoverished in the destination countries. Therefore, stronger connections may increase employment opportunities for the most vulnerable members of society, including women, young people, and those living in poverty. It is necessary to advance justice, peace, and robust institutions in order to achieve economic development objectives. The same holds true for initiatives aimed at promoting tourism. To fully utilise the potential of tourism services for trade and economic growth, the majority of African countries, however, confront substantial obstacles and limitations. In order to help unlock the potential of tourism in Africa and contribute to a structural transformation of the continent's economy, the Economic Development in Africa Report 2017 attempts to identify important bottlenecks and impediments.

It provides policy recommendations on how those barriers and limitations could be addressed. The focus is on the following four challenges:

1.   Strengthening intersectoral linkages.

2.   Enhancing the capacity of tourism to foster more inclusive growth.

3.   Tapping the potential of intraregional tourism through deepening regional integration.

4.   Harnessing peace and stability for tourism.

First, African nations may use the tourism industry's dynamism to advance structural change. The growth of the middle class and discretionary incomes is partly to blame for the rise in regional demand for tourism services. Better transportation, easier access to visas, and increasing disposable incomes would support this trend and give Africans the resources to travel overseas. Additionally, new tourism industry segments, such as medical tourism, are emerging, which can spur the development and financing of healthcare facilities in places like Ghana, Mauritius, and Nigeria. Africa's tourist industry is dynamic and mostly driven by demand; as a result, it needs government assistance in collaboration with the private sector to grow more developed and competitive. It will be necessary to incorporate the sector into national development plans and the communities concerned in order to attract private investment in collaboration with State of Finance provisions to address sector bottlenecks, ease access for air passengers, basic infrastructure, and skilled labour. Local actors and governments will both play a crucial role.

Governments may again start by simplifying the visa application process and enhancing security, information and communications technology, undeveloped health care, airlines, and transportation infrastructure. Long-term support for operational hotels and competition with global hotel chains are both possible from the local private sector. To ensure that a mix of local and foreign money is used in the ownership and operation of hotels, joint ventures between local businesses and international hotel operators can be encouraged. Local tour operators can offer online booking services to encourage travellers to buy tickets and vacation packages directly from local vendors rather than through foreign tour operators (and so add more fantastic local content to the tourism value chains). As part of their economic diversification initiatives, many African nations can increase their service exports by investing in tourism-related infrastructure, which has a critical employment impact. Direct public procurement procedures can open up prospects for more labour-intensive activities in hotels, airports, roads, and other construction projects. Local technology and small businesses have a considerably larger potential to create jobs, particularly in rural areas where tourism is common, and construction activities utilise local materials. Waste management is another neglected (and frequently underfunded) yet essential issue, particularly when a mass tourist or ecologically conscious expansion is envisioned, even though it is a labour-intensive job.

Additionally, by promoting economic diversification, nations can lessen leakages from the tourism sector. The transfer of financial benefits from the industry to local communities is facilitated by creating strong intersectoral linkages, with incomes from employment and business opportunities helping to improve livelihoods and reduce poverty. This is essential to ensuring a more incredible capture of tourist expenditures. There is potential for African nations to use intersectoral tourist links to boost the growth of resilient upstream industries, not just in the services sector but also in some manufacturing and agricultural sectors. Given the extent of variation, intersectoral tourism links must consider sector- and country-level settings. While the value chain's input-output structure affects intersectoral relationships with tourism, a supportive policy environment is still essential for creating economic diversity, supporting local sourcing, and promoting local value addition. The success of current national strategies (for trade, finance, investment, technology, and job creation) in fostering economic growth, which depends in part on multisectoral investment and technical advancement at the national level, would be the main focus of such a policy framework. Growth, employment, innovation, and commerce are all driven by productive investment.

As highlighted, "finance is critically needed to provide firms with the capital they need to develop and facilitate private and public investments in infrastructure, plants and equipment to foster greater competitiveness" UNCTAD (2016a); as UNCTAD has noted, reaching the levels of development needed to fulfil the Sustainable Development Goals. Also, achieving the continent's agreed long-term Agenda 2063 goals will require action by all development partners acting together in a revitalised Global Partnership for Sustainable Development (UNCTAD, 2016b).

Furthermore, tourism can promote more inclusive growth, provided the right legislative framework is in place. Fighting poverty requires promoting respectable work in both formal and unofficial economies. The tourist sector can give significant prospects for the disadvantaged due to its labour-intensive character and a higher possibility that expenditure will benefit the impoverished. Additionally, rural areas, where the majority of people experiencing poverty are concentrated, have a comparative advantage in attracting tourists since the locals may be well-positioned to provide popular tourism activities like music, handicrafts, and excursions. Connections between local suppliers and communities must be established to integrate low-income people into the tourism value chain adequately. Given the youth of Africa's population, youth unemployment is another grave worry. While tourism is critical in creating opportunities for young people, a major problem for the industry is linking young people's education and talents to jobs that are accessible. They will be made by active efforts to improve hospitality and tourism schools. More employable in this industry while also benefiting tourism businesses, who frequently foot the bill for employee training. These methods would be improved by further initiatives to encourage greater occupational skill training, such as unofficial apprenticeship programs. Vertical segregation, unequal pay, discrimination, and less access to financing and education provide challenges for women, who frequently work in the most risky and poorly compensated occupations. But compared to other industries, women who work in tourism tend to have better prospects. In exchange, women provide the tourism industry with important advantages. Promoting female participation in the industry can increase product diversity and promote the preservation of regional cultures and landscapes. In order to enhance the number of jobs open to women and their prospects of promotion, as well as to improve working conditions for women in lower positions, it is possible to expand female involvement through offering training. Additionally, it's important to support female entrepreneurs in better utilising their skills to drive industry innovation and expansion.

African governments should also prioritise accelerating the growth of regional and continental tourism. Africa's intraregional tourism is growing and has chances for export diversification, provided its potential is recognised at the national and regional financial levels. The free movement of people and the liberalisation of air transportation services are two areas in which African nations would profit. Such a development would boost the accessibility of tourism destinations and their ability to compete. Furthermore, countries and local economic communities need to develop comprehensive planning for this tourism sector. Governments should ensure that special attention is given to tourism as the talks for establishing a continental free trade area for goods and services advance, as it makes up a sizeable portion of Africa's trade in services exports. It will be necessary to develop regional integrated tourism policies to be implemented in a concerted manner across regional economic communities and a continental tourism platform to set service standards and coordinate supportive frameworks between regions to ensure Africa's improved competitiveness in the global tourism industry if tourism is to, as envisaged in Agenda 2063, help increase Africa's share of the global trade in goods and services. Creating new goods exclusively for the African market could support those mentioned above. This policy would necessitate a change in emphasis to emphasise African tourists' values and preferences. Regional cooperation in crisis management is also essential to expanding the tourism industry and maintaining peace. Countries should develop thorough multi-stakeholder planning and crisis management processes (such as tight security around tourist destinations and the availability of safe shelter for tourists) to combat the hazards connected with political instability. If efforts to revive the industry after a catastrophe (for instance, through infrastructure finance and new marketing campaigns) are to be effective, countries must incorporate tourism in national disaster management plans through suitable national and regional agencies. There is a reason for more aggressive regional efforts to bring about peace. Political upheaval can have cross-border consequences on tourism, particularly when a country is included in a larger itinerary and travellers switch from one destination country to another.

Similarly, to meet the goals of the African Tourism Strategy of Agenda 2063, Africa should keep increasing levels of investment in the tourism industry. The New Partnership for Africa's Development and the African Union prioritise tourism to alter the continent's economy. In order to promote sustainable tourism, Africa adopted the Tourism Action Plan of the New Partnership for Africa's Development in 2004. The full implementation of an African tourism strategy and the creation of an African tourism organisation was subsequently envisaged in the First Ten-Year Implementation Plan 2014–2023 of Agenda 2063, with a target to at least double the contribution of tourism to GDP in real terms from 2014–2023. It won't be easy to meet the goal by 2023, considering that tourism's overall contribution to GDP climbed from 6.1 per cent in 1995 to 8.3 per cent in 2015, with a peak of 9.9 per cent in 2007. At this rate, the tourism industry would need to expand far more quickly than the GDP and than it did in recent years following the global financial crisis. The suggestions made in this paper are meant to assist in achieving the goals of an African tourist strategy under Agenda 2063. Finally, the dearth of tourism statistics must be addressed immediately. This strategy might be used as a part of ongoing initiatives to enhance the collection of macroeconomic data. To effectively measure the sector's contribution to social and economic development, African governments must create and practice efficient data collection methods for the tourism industry in conjunction with development partners. However, many nations have a chronic lack of fundamental tourism statistics. Little is known about the distribution of these effects or how they may be strengthened, nor is there much data on how various aspects of the tourism industry contribute to its overall influence. It is still difficult to adequately disaggregate available data to ascertain how economic impact varies by kind of visitor, type of tourism, or the sector's structure due to the size of data needed for evaluating supply- and demand-related aggregates. Data on tourism activities broken down by gender are scarce, and measurements of the continent's cross-border commerce flows (a subgroup of business visitors) have been inconsistent. The fact that the business is not classified as an industry in traditional economic accounts further contributes to the difficulty of accurately measuring the consequences of tourism policy studies. The need for improved data and greater government quantitative and monetary policy analysis of the sector is highlighted, as was before indicated.

The fact that only ten African nations currently generate $1 billion or more in annual tourism revenues highlights the enormous market growth potential on the continent. In addition, the area's natural resources and untapped cultural and historical resources present numerous opportunities to draw tourists. However, given that most Africans are relatively low-income, bringing in tourists from other parts of the world is crucial for industry growth. The strongest investment possibilities include nations with well-developed travel infrastructure, reasonably open international movement rules, a desirable environment for launching a tourism-related enterprise, and the possibility of capitalising on natural and cultural endowments. As of 2011, South Africa ($6.1 billion), Kenya ($404 million), Ghana ($270 million), and Uganda ($165 million) were the top recipients of foreign investment in Africa that were primarily focused on the travel and tourism sector. However, particularly in the North African nations and South Africa, some of the region's main tourist markets have seen a decline in recent years. In the meantime, a few frontier markets are developing into more desirable vacation spots for travellers and investors alike due to recognising the potential for tourism-driven development, encouraging investment in the industry, and constructing essential travel infrastructure. This article summarises the top tourist destinations in Africa based on various metrics of the viability of the tourism industry: The investment potential in Morocco, South Africa, Kenya, and Mauritius appears to be favourable. Morocco has been referred to as the "new star of emerging markets among overseas property developers" for several reasons. In addition to the fact that the country has fared better than its neighbours in terms of the political unrest brought on by the Arab Spring, the government has actively and strategically prioritised the tourism sector as a tool for growth—first as part of its Vision 2010 and later updated and included in its Vision 2020. By 2020, the program hopes to double Morocco's current annual tourist count of only 4.3 million in 2000. Egypt was eclipsed by Morocco in 2013 as the top tourist destination in North Africa. It now hosts more than 10 million tourists annually, second only to South Africa on the continent. Government-led tourist development has had two effects. First, in line with a larger worldwide phenomenon known as "Riad fever," foreign capital has flooded Morocco's historical hubs, particularly Marrakech, Fez, Meknes, Casablanca, and Rabat, many of which include medinas that have been designated as UNESCO World Heritage Sites. Second, in addition to cultural hubs, the government has worked to include coastal beach resorts in its list of tourism destinations. Notably, a multilateral agreement that liberalised international air travel between Morocco and the nations that make up the European Union was reached in December 2006. As a result, Morocco is particularly alluring for tourism investors due to its wealth of natural and cultural resources and its welcoming business environment. However, Morocco does not display the same level of price competitiveness as some of its North African rivals, and there is still a significant amount of potential for development in areas that could profit from direct policy reform, such as global openness. Kenya's tourism industry has a lot of room to grow since it only receives slightly more than one million people annually and generates less than $2 billion in income. In light of its natural assets, Kenya, like its neighbour Tanzania, is a stunning market for investment; it is ranked 15th on the scale that assesses natural capital, particularly its well-known safari parks and UNESCO World Heritage sites. Although there is still much space for development, Tanzania, its neighbour in East Africa, performs far worse in terms of the infrastructure for travel and the business climate for the tourism industry. The Kenyan government has actively prioritised the tourist industry as a growth engine, ranking higher than any other nation in sub-Saharan Africa (21st globally) on the metric that assesses the degree to which a given country has prioritised tourism. Approximately 7% of the annual government budget is set up for expanding the tourist sector, including legislation changes that have enhanced conservation and environmental sustainability initiatives and successful marketing activities. Until recently, sugar exports were the main source of income for the small island nation of Mauritius. However, due to the government's forward-thinking and proactive policy planning, its economy has diversified into niche sectors, particularly those for textiles and services. With more than a million visitors per year— roughly the same as Kenya—Mauritius is one of the top African tourism markets in revenue today. One of the main businesses in the nation, tourism contributed 16% of government investment and nearly 30% of overall export revenue in 2015, or $1.68 billion. The Mauritian government has the highest rating in Africa for its prioritisation of tourism, demonstrating the sector's significance. It has led to the developing of a rather advanced infrastructure for land and maritime transit. The principal means of travel into the nation, the air infrastructure, and the business climate for promoting tourism, environmental sustainability, and conservation need significant development. As the nation hosted the 2010 World Cup, the tourist industry flourished, sparking a massive effort to build stadiums that could host large events, festivals, and conferences, potentially luring more business and leisure travel. With total earnings valued at more than $9 billion in 2015 and about 9 million people coming to the country each year, South Africa's tourism industry remains the largest on the continent by volume, despite a decrease from its peak during the World Cup. In particular, the "Big 7" wildlife marketing campaign has been extremely effective, which promotes both the "Big 5" animals common to many safari-promoting countries—lions, leopards, elephants, rhinos, and buffalos—with the addition of whales and great white sharks. According to the World Economic Forum, "South Africa now receives the highest global ranking (53rd) among all African countries for averaged natural (23rd) and cultural (19th) resources" (World Economic Forum on Africa (2017, p.43). Although the South African economy has suffered setbacks in recent years, with inflation rates outpacing per capita income growth, the resulting weakness of the rand against major international currencies has been a positive development in terms of price competitiveness, which is already among the most favourable on the continent (and ranked 43rd worldwide). From the perspective of investors, according to the Travel and Tourism Competitiveness Report (2017), South Africa's tourism business environment (21st in the world) is "characterised by little red tape and modest administrative burden and relatively good infrastructure compared to neighbouring countries." (Travel and Tourism Competitiveness Report,2017). Domestic hospitality companies have flourished, and the largest of these, Tourvest Holdings, now has operations throughout Africa. On the other hand, the country's current travel limitations are the biggest obstacle to the expansion of South African tourism: It is ranked 110th in the world for international openness, and what's worse is that there are signs that soon, new immigration legislation may be passed that might make border controls much stricter. The South African minister of tourism claims that despite recent changes in the visa application procedure that enhanced traveller access to Africa, there has been a significant increase in Chinese visitors. Only 6.5% of the nation's total land area is currently protected, indicating that the government still has a long way to go in prioritising preserving its priceless natural resources. South Africa's ability to maintain its competitiveness and continue drawing large amounts of FDI related to the tourist industry in the future will be significantly influenced by a clear and progressive policy posture prioritising the interests of the tourism sector.

The migration of people to locations outside their typical area for personal, business, or professional reasons is tourism, a social, cultural, and economic phenomenon. In other words, travel for leisure, business, family, or religious reasons, often lasting for a short time, is referred to as tourism. The government and NGOs should educate the public about the value and necessity of tourism. The government should see to it that stringent anti-poaching legislation is upheld. It should be done to advertise widely via stamps, posters, movies, and online media. The appropriate authorities should forbid burning in regions close to national parks and game reserves and should actively discourage it. Governments should improve security in their nations to draw in more tourists. It is crucial to upgrade the roads and other transportation options that lead to popular tourist destinations.

Sports and entertainment must replace conventional national parks and game reserve tourism destinations. The political climate and international relations must be addressed to enable people to move freely between states. In order to keep peace and security worldwide, there must be more international collaboration and effort in the battle against both internal and foreign terrorism. The abovementioned course is significant since tourism depends on world peace and stability. Developing wildlife groups and tourism education centres is necessary to raise awareness of tourism and its attractions. Both domestic and international companies should promote investments in contemporary tourism facilities like hotels and lodges. Industry managers, wardens, travel agents, and guides must receive thorough training to deliver good services. Encourage ecotourism to get the community's complete cooperation in protecting tourist sites, resulting in sustainable tourism. To entice visitors from outside the nation to explore the country's many tourist attractions, some immigration procedures, such as those for issuing visas, should be relaxed. Encourage ecotourism to get the community's complete cooperation in protecting tourist sites, resulting in sustainable tourism. There is no shortage of things you may take part in or locations you can visit for a relaxed weekend, from travelling up north to Mole National Park to Kakum and the Castles on Cape Coast to experiencing the different festivals throughout the year. How frequently do you leave Accra?

I don't mean visiting your birthplace because of duties like family visits, but instead, going somewhere else for fun. Unfortunately, intra-Ghana travel is rare despite Ghana's relatively modest size and abundant beauty that can be found nationwide. Why is this happening, exactly? I have lived in Ghana for six, almost seven years, and throughout that time, I have been to practically every region and visited several tourist attractions. Whether travelling by plane or tour bus was challenging, consider this: In Ghana, there aren't many airports, so if you fly there, you'll almost certainly have to retake the road to get to any place outside the major cities, and you'll be in for a wild trip. When you finally reach your destination, the views and sights you will witness will make you forget entirely about the journey! You'll be anxious to schedule several other excursions throughout Ghana in the following months when that time comes. By then, you'll ask why you didn't know such splendour existed in Ghana. You'll be exhausted from the drive home, the complete anticlimax to such an amazing trip. Given how stunning Ghana is, a few things may be done to enhance tourism there and make it more practical and alluring. The Site's upkeep is essential. It's normal to find websites that have deteriorated over time due to poor supervision. Let's preserve the magnificent natural beauty that is an integral part of Ghana's spirit by offering all-inclusive packages once more and cooperating with other neighbourhood companies to provide a nature experience, food, and bed and breakfast. Culture must be incorporated. Ghana's culture is at the heart of its past, present, and future and is increasingly being incorporated into all facets of travel.

MAKING POLYTECHNICS AND TRAINING COLLEGES ATTRACTIVE TO ESTABLISH A BALANCE IN THE EDUCATIONAL SECTOR IN AFRICA

In the UK, polytechnics have been around since the eighteenth century, but they rose to prominence in the 1960s. Their primary goal was to support industrialisation by supplying a competent technical and engineering workforce. They differed from universities in many respects, including the considerably lower entry requirements and the focus on sub-degree programs that were more vocationally and practically oriented and less academically difficult. Polytechnics had strong ties to business, and the little research they did was highly practical. The "binary divide" in higher education is the distinction between universities and polytechnics. Later, UK Polytechnics began offering degree programs, but since they lacked the authority to confer degrees, another independent body granted their degrees. The United Kingdom's polytechnics were transformed into universities that provide degrees in 1992. The UK was transitioning to a service-oriented economy and required more graduates, which was one motivation for this initiative to increase

opportunities for socially disadvantaged students to pursue higher education. Although many have claimed that the distinction between colleges founded before and after 1992 never truly vanished, this course effectively ended the binary division. When the majority of the former British colonies in Africa gained their independence in the 1950s and 1960s, they adopted a binary higher education system akin to that which was in place in the UK, and both polytechnics and universities were established. The polytechnics were previously known as colleges of advanced technical education until 1979, when they were renamed technikons. With considerable support from the apartheid administration, South Africa established Africa's most cutting-edge higher education system. In 1993, South Africa permitted all of its technikons to offer degree programs and grant degrees, possibly in response to what was happening in the United Kingdom. They yet maintained a practical outlook and distinguished themselves from academic institutions. They gained a reputation or being model institutes for high-quality technical education both locally and globally. As the first African nation to do so, South Africa made a significant step in 2004 when it opted to turn all its technikons into universities. Others were combined with already-existing universities, while others evolved into technology universities. Many academics and higher education policy experts in South Africa and overseas thought that decision was incorrect since they thought the technikons were crucial to the nation's economic growth. Other African nations did the same. A law to transform Ghana's ten polytechnics into technical universities by September 2016 was proposed in 2007. It was extensively disputed throughout the nation, and some esteemed Ghanaian academics opposed it. However, the government moved through in August 2016, and six of the ten polytechnics were turned into universities. Kenya also converted a number of its technical and polytechnic schools into universities. With Africa's largest post-secondary education market, Nigeria is also converting its polytechnics. The Commonwealth Association of Technical Universities and Polytechnics in Africa, formerly known as the Commonwealth The Association of Polytechnics in Africa (CAPA) has changed its name. What is concerning is that there is a significant skills gap in human resources because, in the majority of countries, no new institutions have been established or are being developed to replace the upgraded polytechnics. The relevance of polytechnic education can be evaluated by looking at the engineering field. It is generally acknowledged that for the engineering industry to operate effectively, there must be many more technicians than professional engineers, with an optimum ratio of 1:5 between the two. Estimates suggest that, in a wide range of engineering specialities, the ratio in Africa is of the order of 1:1 or 1:1.5; however, precise statistics on the employment situation in engineering in African countries are not yet accessible. The ratio could worsen when these nations upgrade their polytechnic institutions to university rank. This demonstrates the severe lack of engineering technicians, which has caused graduate engineers to be underemployed and forced to work as technicians in many nations. Unquestionably, Africa needs a larger pool of excellent professional engineers. Still, it also requires an even larger number of technically skilled, adaptable technicians to assist the professional engineers and service and launch small- and medium-scale industries to generate employment, enhance the quality of life, and make better use of local resources. The status of technicians, however, is a significant restriction. One of the reasons for the trend to elevate polytechnics and technical colleges to the status of universities is that they are considered engineers. Sub-Saharan Africa is in a difficult situation because, on the one hand, it has the lowest post-secondary education enrollment of any area in the world (it is currently at 9%). As a result, it is under extreme pressure to raise enrolment, which it does either by increasing university admissions or by founding new universities, typically by modernising its current polytechnics. On the other hand, graduate unemployment is a significant issue that affects almost all African nations. However, specific statistics on its prevalence in various nations are missing. There is no proof that university graduates would have greater employment prospects than those from polytechnic institutions. Contrarily, polytechnic institutions are better equipped to meet Africa's current requirement for a trained middle management and technical workforce. Therefore, it is debatable why polytechnics should be turned into universities. Mauritius is one nation that is actively reconsidering its polytechnic policy. At the start of the twenty-first century, two state universities and two polytechnics existed in Mauritius. In order to carry out the government policy of "one graduate per family," the two polytechnics were combined in 2010 to form a single university. An open university was also created by establishing three new public university campuses in various locations. The latter choice was, however, overturned by a newly elected government in 2015, which determined that the three university sites would be used to establish polytechnics rather than universities. The country's severe lack of intermediate management and technical capabilities, impeding the growth of the small and medium firm sector, and the rising graduate unemployment rate were the two key factors influencing that choice. Although there has to be a huge increase in post-secondary enrollment in Africa, it shouldn't just happen at universities. Africa's progress depends on the tertiary education sector being differentiated. While universities will still be essential to Africa's growth, polytechnics also have a significant impact that must be acknowledged. Therefore, African countries need to critically rethink their plan to convert their polytechnics into universities or establish suitable institutions to replace the converted polytechnics, as Mauritius did. Before significantly revising their tertiary education sector policy, African countries should thoroughly assess the skills required in their priority development areas. It is a difficult endeavour that hardly any African nations have undertaken. The World Bank helps many African nations conduct such an evaluation as part of its Partnership for Skills in Applied Sciences, Engineering, and Technology (PASET) programme in collaboration with the Korea Development Institute.

In Ghana, however, polytechnics are post-secondary institutions that give students the technical training required by industry. The polytechnic's Higher National A diploma (HND) program lasts three years, while universities' first degrees require four years. Legislation encouraging the transition from polytechnics to universities was passed in 2013 after the Ghanaian government thought it would be appropriate to transform polytechnics into technical schools. Polytechnic-university migration is being pursued to enhance the teaching of advanced technical skills in Technical and Vocational Education and Training (TVET) and provide technical and vocational students from second-cycle institutions with more incredible options for progression. Across the country, the movement elicited a range of reactions. Some social groups supported it, while others disapproved. Some people opposed the project because they believed it was poorly thought through, poorly organised, and only a deliberate attempt by the government in power at the time to achieve political advantage. The thoughts above were partly expressed due to the polytechnics becoming technical universities only a few months before the general election. Due to the importance of accessibility for education, polytechnics were strategically positioned around the country, with one facility in each of the ten regions. The names of these institutions, such as the Accra Polytechnic in Accra, the regional capital of the Greater Accra Region, and the Ho Polytechnic in Ho, the regional capitals, inspired the regional capital of the Volta Region. Beginning with the 2016–17 academic year, eight of Ghana's ten polytechnics have already been granted the status of technical universities. The two remaining polytechnics will be reevaluated and granted university status once they fulfil the requirements and standards. Among the institutions that have been given the title of technical university are Ho Technical University, Accra Technical University, Cape Coast Technical University, Kumasi Technical University, Takoradi Technical University, Sunyani Technical University, Koforidua Technical University and Tamale Technical University. The institutes that do not yet have the title of technical university are Wa Polytechnic and Bolgatanga Polytechnic. Dr George Afeti, a former rector of Ho Technical University (previously Ho Polytechnic) and a former secretary general of the Commonwealth Association of Polytechnics in Africa, said polytechnics shouldn't become traditional universities with similar missions or duplicate the courses and programs those institutions already offered after gaining university status. Even before polytechnics were converted into technical universities, the issue of equality between them and traditional public institutions has long existed. Teachers were concerned about employment conditions, but students were worried about finding work after graduation. As a result of their degrees being seen as "better equipped" for occupations, some claim that graduates from traditional colleges were paid more than those from polytechnic institutions. The polytechnic institute's students were concerned about this. Will this be considered during the migration? Time will only tell. Another problem was that some traditional universities forbade applicants from polytechnic institutions to transfer HND credits toward first-degree programs in the same programs they had finished at the polytechnic. If credit transfer is allowed, students will not be required to enrol in the first year; instead, they will only need to finish their studies in three years if a credit transfer is not allowed. It is possible to view the switch from polytechnics to universities as a strategic repositioning effort to benefit students and improve the image of polytechnics (now known as technical universities). Polytechnic students reportedly believe that shifting will grant them the same reputation and perks accorded to university students in the country. Education and training are necessary for productive employment and economic and social advancement. Therefore, it is predicted that Ghana's tertiary education reforms will promote the growth of industry-specific talents. Once more, secondary school students may enrol in junior college to pursue a general education or a polytechnic to pursue a more specialised education after finishing their O-level exams. Many students enrol in junior institutions because they are unclear about their preferred careers. Another aspect is the extra year needed to complete polytechnic studies. While some institutions allow the mapping of polytechnic modules, the process can be difficult. This is done so that a polytechnic student who has already studied a particular module can avoid retaking it in to save time. Polytechnic education is crucial since Singapore places a lot of emphasis on a digital economy based on skills. Polytechnic education also better prepares students for post-secondary study by letting them concentrate on building their fundamental skills in extremely specialised programs. It is time to reorganise polytechnic education to make it more interesting to students. Allowing polytechnic students who perform well in their classes to complete their studies in two years, much like junior college students, would be one way to help them obtain their tertiary degrees more quickly. A potential solution may be to provide secondary school students with several options to participate in polytechnic courses. This course can be completed by scheduling lectures at polytechnic institutions all summer to increase student awareness of the variety of options available. The federal government has been recommended to create initiatives to draw students to polytechnics and colleges of education by Prof. Attahiru Jega, a former INEC chairman. Jega emphasised the need for such policies to solve concerns with educational access during the Federal University of Dutse's first convocation speech on Saturday in Jigawa. Jega noted an increase in university applicants in his speech at the Federal University, Dutse, titled "Reforming the Nigerian Tertiary Education Sector: Challenges and Prospects." The demand for polytechnics, colleges of education, and mono-technics was lower among tertiary candidates than among university applications. Access to education must be improved together with initiatives to draw students to other tertiary institutions. Only Forty-five thousand of the over 1.3 million university applicants in 2010 intended to attend polytechnics and colleges of education. Jega stated that despite the entry of new private universities, the demand for higher education did not significantly decline. On the other side, there was a revelation at the 4th Pan African Youth Forum, held in Victoria Falls and hosted by the Association of Technical Universities and Polytechnic in August, that "it is sad that opportunities for applicants to pursue higher education are contracting rather than expanding and that demand is rising while access is declining. A paradigm shift is necessary to revive TVET for employment creation rather than job hunting, according to the guest of honour, Mr Madi Ousman Jatta, Deputy Permanent. Secretary for the Ministry of Higher Education in the Gambia. He said that strong public-private partnerships between the government, industry, educational institutions and the employer are required in order to revive TVET for employment creation rather than job hunting. ATUPA was established in 2019 by a resolution passed by the General Assembly of Heads of Member Institutions of the Commonwealth Association of Technical Universities and Polytechnics in Africa in Kigali, Rwanda, and ratified by the Ministers of Education of African Union member states at the 3rd Ordinary Session of the Specialized Committee on Education, Science, and Technology. The first youth forum took place in Nigeria's Abuja, the second in Rwanda's Kigali, and the third took place virtually due to the Covid-19 lockdown. Zimbabwe is hosting the fourth edition, and the forum's goal is to give young people a place to interact, share ideas, and develop their entrepreneurial abilities to move the continent forward. TVET holds the key to technological advancement, quick industrialisation, wealth creation, and poverty reduction as a catalyst for socio-economic development, according to Tafadzva Mudondo, principal engineer at Harare Polytechnic and vice chairwoman of the Southern and Central African Region of ATUPA. He claimed that the continent is blessed with natural resources not used to the motherland's advantage. Despite having a lot of skills, Africa is regarded as developing. Therefore, we must alter how we instruct our kids and limit their perspectives to foster a business-minded attitude. "Our educational system needs to be changed to solve our issues and produce young people with the same views as everyone else. Eng says these young people should launch their businesses as examples of civic engagement and entrepreneurial energy. He said that TVET is crucial for developing the resilience required to sustain economic progress in young people. The government formerly supported the Education 5.0 program, which seeks to foster innovation at educational institutions. This is compatible with the Second Republic's commitment to transform the economy through human capital development. "TVET produces youth who are the future practitioners in engineering, leadership, and entrepreneurship designed to mitigate against socio-economic challenges and national development agenda," added Eng Mudondo. The summit, according to ATUP Secretary General Jahou Faal, strives to find ways to make money and provide for young people's livelihoods so they may boost the continent's gross domestic product. Economic development, decent employment, and economic growth are crucial building blocks for reducing poverty in Africa and achieving the Agenda 2063 goals of the Africa Union. However, in Ghana, 38 publicly owned Teacher Training Institutions (TTIs) that offered certificate programs to prepare teachers for primary schools were given university status and renamed Colleges of Education (COEs) to offer post-secondary degrees in 2008. TTIs have encountered several issues that have jeopardised their ability to maintain their position as tertiary institutions after being raised and re-designated as Colleges of Education. These concerns, which touch on governance, regulation, management, and college autonomy, must be thoroughly assessed in order to help the institutions successfully carry out their mandate. In order to promote both individual growth and the creation of human capital for global socio-economic development, education is essential. In order to prepare people to support the teaching and learning process in schools, teacher education is essential. Teacher education is crucial in preparing individuals to facilitate schools' teaching and learning process. The European Union (2012) determined that "within educational institutions, teaching professionals are the most important determinants of how learners will perform; and it is what teachers know, do and care about that matters." (The European Union 2012). In Ghana over the past forty years, teacher education in Ghana has undergone several modifications. These modifications result from policy changes to produce well-trained teachers to meet the country's educational needs at various times. "These changes have produced different cohorts of teachers with different types of certificates" (Anamuah-Mensah, 2006). "Colleges of Education (formerly known as Teacher Training Institutes) initially offered 2-year Post-Middle Certificate "B" programs, followed by 4-year Post-Middle Certificate "A" and 2-year Post–Secondary Certificate "A" programs. The 2-year program was later extended to a 3-year program, which ran alongside the 4-year certificate "A" programs until it was curtailed in the 1980s." (Addo-Obeng, 2008). Following a thorough examination of Ghana's educational system, the government released a White Paper in the early 2000s. In accordance with this decree, "all Teacher Training Colleges will be upgraded into diploma-awarding institutions and be affiliated with the education-oriented universities" (Government of Ghana, 2004). Regarding this, 38 Teacher Training Colleges that operated in 2008 as Colleges of Education (COE) to provide post-secondary education were re-designated as Teacher Training Colleges (TTC) to operate at a level similar to level 4 of the International System of Classification of Education (ISCED

4). The former Teacher's Training Institutions (TTIs), which are now designated as tertiary institutions, were once part of the Ghana Education Service (GES). This organisation is in charge of pre-tertiary education. One of the sections of the Ghana Education Service, the Teacher Education Division, directly oversaw the TTIs. Therefore, GES was in charge of funding, hiring staff, and deciding what was necessary to enrol in the universities. However, the Institute of Education at the University of Cape Coast has evaluated and certified TTIs' output. The Teacher Education Division and the Institute of Education have worked together throughout the years to establish and continuously assess Ghana's pre-university teacher education curriculum (Opare, 2008). Act 847, the Colleges of Education Act, was passed in 2012 to support the institutions' new status formally. In order to regulate tertiary education institutions in Ghana, the National Council for Tertiary Education (NCTE) has been given control over the universities. Since being reclassified as COEs in 2008, TTIs have had difficulties concerning governance, infrastructure, monitoring, and autonomy. Therefore, this article examines the difficulties the Colleges of Education confront in establishing their new status as higher educational institutions. Additionally, suggestions are made to help Colleges of Education become more desirable options for tertiary education in Ghana. The improvement of teacher preparation through the elevation of TTIs to Colleges of Education portends well for Ghana's educational system. Indeed, ensuring high-quality outcomes in basic education depends on the preparation of highly qualified teachers. According to the previous analysis, several obstacles prevent colleges of education from smoothly transitioning into post-secondary institutions. Colleges of education should have greater autonomy to promote administrative and leadership innovation in beginning teacher preparation. In order to "chaperone." As they transition from non-tertiary to tertiary institutions, individuals with experience in the governance of tertiary education institutions should be selected. Additionally, the Colleges' top management team should be trained in the abilities needed to oversee tertiary institutions of learning. The National Council for Tertiary Education ought to support the development of the governing councils' capacity to improve the members' knowledge of tertiary education institution governance. The Council needs to set up management development courses for the Colleges' top management staff. The National Council for Tertiary Education has to improve the way it oversees and regulates colleges of education. Policies, standards, and norms need to be developed immediately to enable efficient monitoring and evaluation of changes in the Colleges. The clause in Section 19 of the Colleges of Education Act, 2012, which states that statutes passed by college governing councils must receive the minister of education's approval, would compromise the independence of the institutions and stall the implementation of the councils' decisions. Additionally, political meddling in the administration and management of the Colleges will result. The National Council for Tertiary Education has to improve how it oversees and regulates colleges of education. Policies, standards, and norms need to be developed immediately to enable efficient monitoring and evaluation of changes in the Colleges. The clause in Section 19 of the Colleges of Education Act, 2012, which states that statutes passed by college governing councils must receive the minister of education's approval, would compromise the independence of the institutions and stall then implementation of the councils' decisions. Additionally, political meddling in the administration and management of the Colleges will result. The Colleges of Education Act of 2012 also specifies in section 4 that governing boards of colleges of education shall "ensure that basic and action research forms part an integral part of teacher education to promote quality teaching and learning in the classroom," however, this seems far-fetched. Colleges of Education operate at ISCED level 5 and lack the material and human resources required to conduct basic research. The Colleges shouldn't use their meagre resources to carry out fundamental research. In fact, the country would benefit more if colleges of education were recognised as teaching institutions to maintain their core mission of educating teachers for elementary schools. Despite the foregoing, institutions should develop their capacity to do action research so that teachers can document their real-world experiences. The Colleges of Education Act, section 4(b), states that a college of education shall "decide on the subjects to be taught based on their special relevance to the needs of the educational system... and national development, "in contrast to the current practice of assigning specific subject areas to colleges of education in order to facilitate the preparation of generalist and specialist teachers to meet national development goals. The supply of specialised and generalist teachers may become unbalanced if individual colleges apply Section 4b of the Colleges of Education Act, which would be detrimental to the educational system. According to the current author, evaluating the courses offered by colleges of education should consider the entire colleges of education subsector and the market and geographic reach of each institution. The analyses mentioned above serve as the foundation for reviewing the Colleges of Education Act, 2012, in order to clarify the autonomy of colleges of education and establish clear policies to guarantee that teachers with a variety of specialities are prepared to satisfy the demands of basic schools in Ghana. The Ghana Education Service has employed many untrained teachers due to an inadequate number of trained teachers, which is a setback in the country's efforts to prepare an adequate number of teachers for the basic education subsector. This afore-mentioned issue is because Colleges of Education are unable to accept all qualified applicants due to the government's mandatory admission quota for the Colleges. For instance, according to Ministry of Education data, only 44.8% and 66.3% of kindergarten and primary school instructors are qualified (Ministry of Education, 2012). Additionally, several principals have asserted that they could enrol more pupils than the current enrollment if given the opportunity. For instance, it was claimed that the principal of Enchi College of Education that the college could enrol more than 500 students, although its quota has only been set at 170 (Daily Graphic, 2013). In this context, the Ghanaian government ought to consider permitting the universities to enrol a certain proportion of qualified candidates who cannot receive financial aid and enrol as fee-paying students. The bad quality of the infrastructure and the low level of training of most college teachers are other significant issues that must be addressed for them to carry out their duties. Therefore, it is advised that the government of Ghana establish a dedicated fund to give the colleges more facilities and equipment. The government should also help college professors obtain the credentials to teach in higher institutions. Colleges of Education have undergone a long and difficult transformation from post-secondary non-tertiary institutions to tertiary universities. The procedure began in 2008 and will take some time to complete. The Vice-Principal of Our Lady of Apostles Colleges of Education, Reverend Sister Mante summed up the current state of the Colleges of Education in these words: "We are neither firmly entrenched as tertiary institutions nor are we still regarded as post-secondary non-tertiary institutions." Between the two, we are. Even though the National Council for Tertiary Education has governed us for almost four years, the Ghana Education Service continues to oversee the salaries of college employees and promotions. It is encouraging for Ghana's educational system because TTIs have been promoted to Colleges of Education. In order to promote the preparation of quality teachers for the pre-tertiary sector and clear up any confusion regarding the current status of the colleges, stakeholders (Ghana Education Service, National Council for Tertiary Education, and the Ministry of Education) should work together to hasten the completion of the transition from Teacher Training Colleges to Colleges of Education. It is impossible to overstate how important it is to enhance colleges of education in order to diversify tertiary education in Ghana. Two batches of secondary school graduates whose mere numbers exceed the capability of the country's universities and polytechnics have resulted from the decrease in secondary education's length from four years to three years in 2008 following a change in political administration in Ghana. In order for the institutions to gain the necessary personnel and material resources to support the Colleges of Education's positioning, it is required to boost the Colleges of Education financially. Finally, the award of diplomas to training colleges and polytechnics discourages most students from pursuing such institutions compared to Universities that offer degrees as qualifications. The above-stated problem is because in the job environment in Africa, attention is given to stuff more than technical know-how such that the system only recruits graduates with higher qualifications. Had it not been for this argument, students entering the tertiary would have given much thought to the polytechnics and training colleges as they tend to expose their students to a more practical highly and skill-oriented schooling environment. However, the big question is, who even stands a good chance of being employed in Africa, the university graduate or the polytechnics and training college graduates? African leaders should reform the tertiary education in our continent to provide a balance and healthy cooperation among universities, polytechnics and training colleges. Attractive measures should be in place to erode the inferiority complex in students seeking to advance their education endeavours with polytechnics and training colleges. Quality and appropriate funding should also be channelled to these institutions to make it attractive to high-profile instructors, lecturers and activists.

REFERENCES

1. Tsey, K. (2011) Re-thinking Development in Africa. [edition unavailable]. Langaa RPCIG. Available at: https://www.perlego.com/book/541492/rethinking-development-in-africa-an-oral-history-approach-from-botoku-rural-ghana-pdf (Accessed: 14 October 2022).
2. "Globalization and the State: an Overview," Report of the 15th Meeting of Experts on the United Nations Programme in Public Administration and Finance, April 2000
3. Bazerman, Max, and Don A. Moore. <u>Judgment in Managerial Decision Making</u>. 8th ed. John Wiley & Sons, 2013
4. Fisher, Roger, 1922-2012. (1991). Getting to yes : negotiating agreement without giving in. Boston :Houghton Mifflin,
5. Delich, V. (2002) 'Developing Countries and the WTO Dispute Settlement System' in B. Hoekman, A. Mattoo and P. English (eds.), Development, Trade, and the WTO.
6. Cerrex (2002) 'The Usage of the EU Trade Preferences (GSP and Lomé)', a study on behalf of the Department for International Development (mimeo). London: Cerrex Limited.
7. Commission on Intellectual Property Rights (CIPR) (2002) Integrating Intellectual Property Rights and Development Policy. London: CIPR.

8. Armah, Ayi Kwei. "The beautyful ones are not yet born." Oxford, Eng. : Heinemann, 1988, 1968

9. OguejioforJ.Obi. Philosophy and the African Predicament. Ibadan: Hope Publications, 2001

10. Achebe Chinua. 1988. The Trouble with Nigeria, in Gbenga Lawal, 2007, Corruption and Development in Africa: Challenges for Economic and Political Change. Humanity and Social Sciences Journal 2 (1): 01-07-

11. Hugh Bayley MP, Chair of the United Kingdom's House of Commons Africa All Party Parliamentary Group, 29 March 2006, available at http://www.transparency.org/publications/newsletter/2006/may_2006

12. Himmelstrand, Ulf (ed), 1994. "In Search of New Paradigms," in African Perspectives

13. Phillip, Dotun (1999) "Not a Chance" in Globalization And Nigeria"s Economic Development, Plan" paper presented as the AFRC Policy Seminar, Dar-Es-Salaam, Tanzania, February

14. Hamet, P., and Tremblay, J., 2017. Artificial intelligence in medicine. Metabolism 69, S36–S40

15. Adamopoulou, E., and Moussiades, L., 2020. An overview of chatbot technology, in: IFIP International Conference on Artificial Intelligence Applications and Innovations, Springer. pp. 373–383.

16. Gadzala, A., 2018. Coming to life: Artificial intelligence in Africa. Atlantic Council, November 14.

17. Chatterjee, S., and Bhattacharjee, K.K., 2020. Adoption of artificial intelligence in higher education: A quantitative analysis using structural equation modelling. Education and Information Technologies 25, 3443–3463.

18. Borenstein, J., and Howard, A., 2021. Emerging challenges in A.I. and the need for A.I. ethics education. A.I. and Ethics 1, 61–65.

19. Bankole, F.O., Bankole, O.O., and Brown, I., 2011. Mobile banking adoption in Nigeria. The Electronic Journal of Information Systems in Developing Countries 47, 1–23

20. UNWTO (2016). UNWTO Tourism Highlights. Madrid. Available at http://www.eunwto.org/doi/pdf/10.18111/978 9284418145 (accessed March 17 2017).

21. UNCTAD (2016a). Economic Development in Africa Report 2016: Debt Dynamics and Development Finance in Africa. United Nations publication. Sales No. E.16.II.D.3. New York and Geneva.

22. Francesc, P., Miguel, S., Axel, R., and Paula, V., 2019. Artificial intelligence in education: Challenges and opportunities for sustainable development—UNESCO Biblioteca Digital. Technical Report. UNESCO Working Papers on Education Policy. UNESCO. https://unesdoc.unesco.org. UNESCO.

23. Bazerman, Max, and Don A. Moore. Judgment in Managerial Decision Making, 8th. Wiley & Sons, 2012.

24. Fisher, Roger and William Ury. *Getting to Yes: Negotiating Agreement Without Giving In,* 3rd ed. New York, NY: Penguin Books, 2011. <http://www.beyondintractability.org/library/external-resource?biblio=23737>.

25. Arvanitis, Alexios & Antonis, Karampatzos. (2011). Negotiation and Aristotle's Rhetoric: Truth over interests?. Philosophical Psychology. 24. 845-860. 10.1080/09515089.2011.569910.

26. Armah, Ayi Kwei, The Beautyful Ones Are Not Yet Born, Boston: Houghton, Mifflin, 1968 (ASIN: B000JV2N50).

27. Oguejiofor, J. O. (2001). Philosophy and the African Predicament. Ibadan: Hope Publications.

28. Frankl, V. E. (1992). *Man's search for meaning: An introduction to logotherapy* (4th ed.) (I. Lasch, Trans.). Beacon Press.

29. Eddy Maloka 2002, NEPAD and Africa's future https://www.ajol.info/index.php/ai/issue/view/2886 ,https://doi.org/10.4314/ai.v32i2.22290

30. Nanji, Munir and Muchiri,Timothy (2009) "Trade in Sub-Saharan Africa: Where Next?", Citi Nigeria

31. Sindzingre, Alice Nicole, The European Union Economic Partnership Agreements with Sub-Saharan Africa (June 19, 2008). UNU-CRIS Working Paper No. W-2008/5, Available at SSRN: https://ssrn.com/abstract=1836062 or http://dx.doi.org/10.2139/ssrn.1836062

32. Theodore H. Cohn, 2008 Global Political Economy + Mysearchlab, Pearson College Division, 2008, ISBN:0205700659, 9780205700653.

33. Dani Rodrick, The Real Exchange Rate and Economic Growth. 2008. Copy at https://tinyurl.com/yyguuakm

34. Zainal Aznam Yusof & Deepak Bhattasali, 2008. "Economic Growth and Development in Malaysia," World Bank Publications - Books, The World Bank Group, number 28046, December.

35. Stephen V. Faraone, Tobias Banaschewski, David Coghill, Yi Zheng, Joseph Biederman, Mark A. Bellgrove, Jeffrey H. Newcorn, Martin Gignac, Nouf M. Al Saud, Iris Manor, Luis Augusto Rohde, Li Yang, Samuele Cortese, Doron Almagor, Mark A. Stein, Turki H. Albatti, Haya F. Aljoudi, Mohammed M.J. Alqahtani, Philip Asherson, Lukoye Atwoli, Sven Bölte, Jan K. Buitelaar, Cleo L. Crunelle, David Daley, Søren Dalsgaard, Manfred Döpfner, Stacey Espinet (on behalf of CADDRA), Michael Fitzgerald, Barbara Franke, Manfred Gerlach, Jan Haavik, Catharina A. Hartman, Cynthia M. Hartung, Stephen P. Hinshaw, Pieter J. Hoekstra, Chris Hollis, Scott H. Kollins, J.J. Sandra Kooij, Jonna Kuntsi, Henrik Larsson, Tingyu Li, Jing Liu, Eugene Merzon, Gregory Mattingly, Paulo Mattos, Suzanne McCarthy, Amori Yee Mikami, Brooke S.G. Molina, Joel T. Nigg, Diane Purper-Ouakil, Olayinka O. Omigbodun, Guilherme V. Polanczyk,

Yehuda Pollak, Alison S. Poulton, Ravi Philip Rajkumar, Andrew Reding, Andreas Reif, Katya Rubia, Julia Rucklidge, Marcel Romanos, J. Antoni Ramos-Quiroga, Arnt Schellekens, Anouk Scheres, Renata Schoeman, Julie B. Schweitzer, Henal Shah, Mary V. Solanto, Edmund Sonuga-Barke, César Soutullo, Hans-Christoph Steinhausen, James M. Swanson, Anita Thapar, Gail Tripp, Geurt van de Glind, Wim van den Brink, Saskia Van der Oord, Andre Venter, Benedetto Vitiello, Susanne Walitza, Yufeng Wang,

The World Federation of ADHD International Consensus Statement: 208 Evidence-based conclusions about the disorder, Neuroscience & Biobehavioral Reviews, Volume 128,2021, Pages 789-818, ISSN 0149-7634, https://doi.org/10.1016/j.neubiorev.2021.01.0 22.

(https://www.sciencedirect.com/science/article/pii/S014976342100049X)

36. Garcia, Jose. (2015). The Economics and Policy Implications of Infrastructure Sharing and Mutualisation in Africa.
37. Larsson, S. and Heintz, F. (2020). Transparency in artificial intelligence. Internet Policy Review,[online] 9(2). Available at: https://policyreview.info/concepts/transparency-artificial-intelligence.

38. Wang, Yu-Yin & Wang, Yi-Shun. (2019). Development and validation of an artificial intelligence anxiety scale: an initial application in predicting motivated learning behavior. Interactive Learning Environments. 30. 1-16. 10.1080/10494820.2019.1674887.

39. Chatterjee, Sheshadri & Bhattacharjee, Kalyan. (2020). Adoption of artificial intelligence in higher education: a quantitative analysis using structural equation modelling. Education and Information Technologies. 25. 10.1007/s10639-020-10159-7.

40. Chinedu Wilfred Okonkwo, Abejide Ade-Ibijola, Chatbots applications in education: A systematic review, Computers and Education: Artificial Intelligence, Volume 2, 2021, 100033, ISSN 2666-920X, https://doi.org/10.1016/j.caeai.2021.100033.

41. Borenstein, Jason & Howard, Ayanna. (2020). Emerging challenges in AI and the need for AI ethics education. AI and Ethics. 1. 1-5. 10.1007/s43681-020-00002-7.

42. Ruane, Elayne & Birhane, Abeba & Ventresque, Anthony. (2019). Conversational AI: Social and Ethical Considerations.

43. Bankole, Felix & Bankole, Omolola & Brown, Irwin. (2011). Mobile Banking Adoption in Nigeria. 47. 10.1002/j.1681-4835.2011.tb00330.x.

44. Lekhanya, Lawrence. (2013). Cultural Influence On The Diffusion And Adoption Of Social Media Technologies By Entrepreneurs In Rural South Africa. International Business

& Economics Research Journal (IBER). 12. 1563. 10.19030/iber.v12i12.8250.

45. UNCTAD (2016b). Nairobi Maafikiano. From decision to action: Moving towards an inclusive and equitable global economic environment for trade and development. TD/519/Add.2. September 5.

46. Commission on Intellectual Property Rights (CIPR) (2002) Integrating Intellectual Property Rights and Development Policy. London: CIPR.

47. European Commission (EC) (1997) Green Paper on relations between the European Union and the ACP countries on the eve of the 21st century. Luxembourg: Office for Official Publications of the European Communities.

48. Kolawole T. Raheem and Kupari Pekka (Eds.), Educational issues for sustainable development in Africa (pp. 28-40). Lasonen Johana: Institute for Educational Research.

49. Ashby, E. (1966). Universities, British, Indian, African. London: Weidenfeld and Nicolson.

50. Ajayi, JFA, LKH Goma, and G.A. Johnson (1996). The African experience with higher education. Oxford: James Currey Publishers and Accra: The Association of African Universities.

51. Balderston, F.E. (1995). Managing today's universities: Strategies for viability change and excellence. San Francisco: Jossey and Bass. Norwood, NJ: ABLEX Publishing.

52. Berdahl, R. (1990). Academic freedom, autonomy and accountability in British

universities, Studies in Higher Education, 15(2), pp. 169-180.

53. Daily Graphic (2013). Structures underutilised at Enchi College of Education, Daily Graphic April 13, 2013, p. 32.

54. Effah, P., J.A.N. Mensa-Bonsu. (2001). Governance of tertiary education institutions in Ghana, National Council for Tertiary Education.

55. European Union (2012). Supporting the Teaching Professions for Better Learning Outcomes, European Union.

56. Government of Ghana (2002). Meeting education challenges in the twenty-first century: Report of the President's Committee on review of education reforms in Ghana.Accra: Government of Ghana.

57. ----- (2004). White paper on the report of the education reform review committee. Accra: Ministry of Education, Youth and Sports. ----- (2012). Colleges of education act, 2012, Act 847. Accra: Government of Ghana.----- (2012). Constitution of the Republic of Ghana. Ghana: Government of Ghana.

58. Ministry of Education (2012). Education sector performance report. Accra: Ministry of Education. www.yourcommonwealth.org www.straitstimes.com www.dailypost.ng

59. Mohamedbhai,G(2017). The importance of polytechnics for Africa's development, pp. 30-33.

60. Nelson M. Speech, April 1998 Address by President Nelson Mandela at the opening of the Emthonjeni Youth Centre, Pretoria

Available at:
http://www.mandela.gov.za/mandela_speeche s/1998/980825_emthonjeni.htm

61. Dalai Lama [Tenzin Gyatso] and Desmond Tutu. 2016. *The Book of Joy: Lasting Happiness in a Changing World*. With Douglas Abrams. New York: Avery.

62. United Nations (1984), United Nations General Assembly Official Records, 20th Plenary Meeting, Thursday, 4 October 1984, at 10.40 a.m., New York, (A/39/PV.20), pp. 405-410.

63. Arvanitis, Alexios & Antonis, Karampatzos. (2011). Negotiation and Aristotle's Rhetoric: Truth over interests?. Philosophical Psychology. 24. 845-860. 10.1080/09515089.2011.569910.

64. Thompson, Leigh. (2005). The Mind and Heart of The Negotiator.

65. Jack Colwell and Chip Huth (2019) Unleashing the Power Of Unconditional Respect, Routledge, 2019 ISBN: 0367864487, 9780367864484

66. Kofi Annan (2004), .addressing the UNITED NATIONS CONVENTION AGAINST CORRUPTION (Accessed June 2022) site https://www.unodc.org/unodc/en/treaties/CA C/

67. WORLD ECONOMIC FORUM ON AFRICA: Durban Meeting. (2017, June). Africa Research Bulletin: Economic, Financial and Technical Series, 54(4), 21665C-21668A.

https://doi.org/10.1111/j.1467-6346.2017.07644.x

68. https://www.google.com/url?sa=t&rct=j&q=&esrc=s&source=web&cd=&ved=2ahUKEwjymqmkg5mAAxXaiVwKHaHVAzkQFnoECBgQAQ&url=https%3A%2F%2Fwww.weforum.org%2Freports%2Fthe-travel-tourism-competitiveness-report-2017%2F&usg=AOvVaw1Va6ZY-qEHU47QWL6sasp-&opi=89978449. (n.d.). https://www.google.com/url?sa=t&rct=j&q=&esrc=s&source=web&cd=&ved=2ahUKEwjymqmkg5mAAxXaiVwKHaHVAzkQFnoECBgQAQ&url=https%3A%2F%2Fwww.weforum.org%2Freports%2Fthe-travel-tourism-competitiveness-report-2017%2F&usg=AOvVaw1Va6ZY-qEHU47QWL6sasp-&opi=89978449

69. https://www.google.com/url?sa=t&rct=j&q=&esrc=s&source=web&cd=&cad=rja&uact=8&ved=2ahUKEwji9JzwhJmAAxVKTEEAHWwwASsQFnoECA0QAQ&url=https%3A%2F%2Fwww.hrw.org%2Fworld-report%2F2012%2Fcountry-chapters&usg=AOvVaw2AX1vcVAP3rDeLRHGoWonh&opi=89978449. www.google.com/url?sa=t&rct=j&q=&esrc=s&source=web&cd=&cad=rja&uact=8&ved=2ahUKEwji9JzwhJmAAxVKTEEAHWwwASsQFnoECA0QAQ&url=https%3A%2F%2Fwww.hrw.org%2Fworld-report%2F2012%2Fcountry-chapters&usg=AOvVaw2AX1vcVAP3rDeLRHGoWonh&opi=89978449.

70. Anamuah-Mensah, J., Mereku, D. K., & Asabere-Ameyaw, A. (2006). The Contexts for Learning and Instruction Influencing Ghanaian JSS2 Students\'Dismal Performance in TIMSS-2003. *African Journal of Educational Studies in Mathematics and Sciences*, *4*, 15-32.

71. Addo-Obeng 2008"View of the Upgrading of Teacher Training Institutions to Colleges of Education: Issues and Prospects | African Journal of Teacher Education." View of the Upgrading of Teacher Training Institutions to Colleges of Education: Issues and Prospects | African Journal of Teacher Education, journal.lib.uoguelph.ca/index.php/ajote/article/view/2728/3129.

ABOUT THE AUTHOR

Born and raised in Kumasi, Ghana, Enoch Akwasi Kwarteng passionately loves philosophy and intellectualism. He has been featured on various platforms, such as the Sangyin Podcast, where he shared his perspectives on how African youth can take their destiny into their hands to develop themselves and change their narrative for the best. He is the author of books like ***WISDOM IS THE NEW SWAG***: a book that guides one to reconsider the need to consciously develop oneself in both health and wealth, factoring in their mental, emotional and social development; ***and ECHOES OF THE SLEEPING GIANT***: A book filled with personal experiences and research modules and disciplines that answer the fortune of Asia and how some effective practices of China can be applied in Africa to enhance development. He is a software engineer by profession. He has worked as a Microsoft technical support engineer in software companies like Shanghai Wicresoft CO., LTD. He is an alumnus of Zhengzhou University.

9 798885 330444